AF262747

ITTY BITTY INK

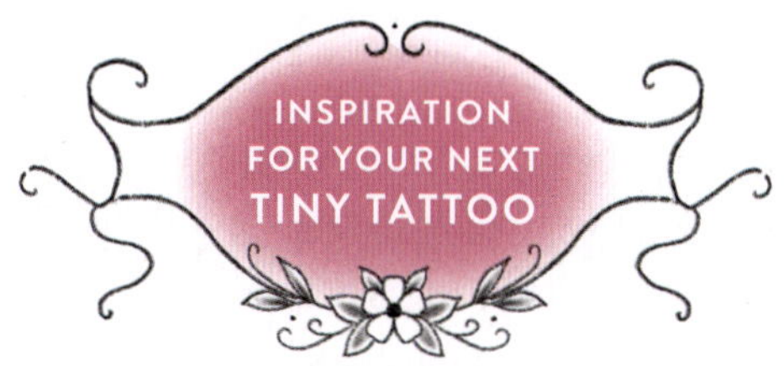

By McKenna Lah

CHRONICLE BOOKS

SAN FRANCISCO

To the girls and the gays:
Thank you for everything.

Library of Congress Cataloging-in-Publication Data available.

ISBN 978-1-7972-3969-9

Manufactured in China.

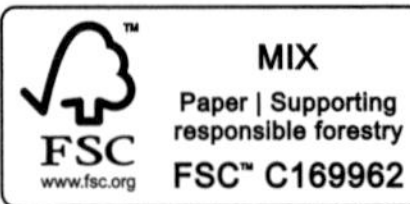

Design by Barbara Bersche.

10 9 8 7 6 5 4 3 2 1

Chronicle books and gifts are available at special quantity
discounts to corporations, professional associations, literacy
programs, and other organizations. For details and discount
information, please contact our premiums department at
corporategifts@chroniclebooks.com or at 1-800-759-0190.

Chronicle Books LLC
680 Second Street
San Francisco, California 94107
www.chroniclebooks.com

CONTENTS

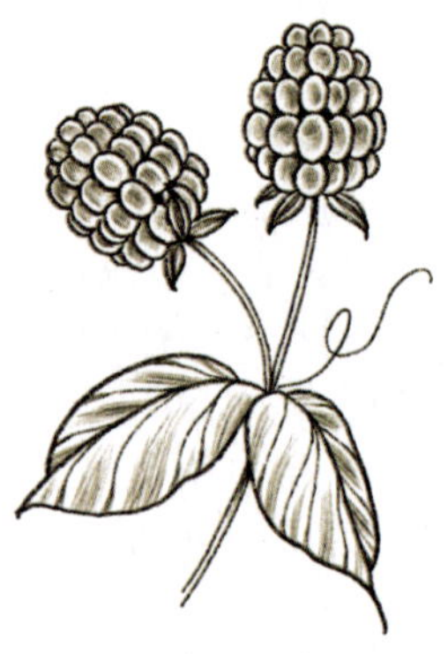

Welcome to *Itty Bitty Ink*, a collection of cute little illustrations to inspire your next tattoo!

My name is McKenna, and I'm a Los Angeles–based tattoo artist. Itty bitty tattoos are the foundation of my tattoo journey. While I was in college, I spent all my free time drawing and tattooing small designs on myself and my (incredibly trusting) friends. I explored the LA tattoo scene as a client while building my portfolio as an artist, and I met so many talented people who specialize in delicate, fine-line tattoos. Once I started working in a shop, I had the opportunity to learn and work among the best, and I met the sweetest clients along the way. I've been tattooing itty bitty designs for five years, and I couldn't be more grateful for the connections I've made through this art form. I've drawn the following pieces with so much love and care, and I hope you find some that resonate with you. Whether it's a cute critter, a blooming flower, a memorable trinket, or your favorite fruit, there's something here for everybody. Enjoy!

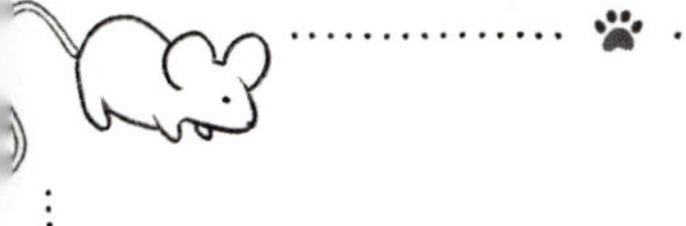 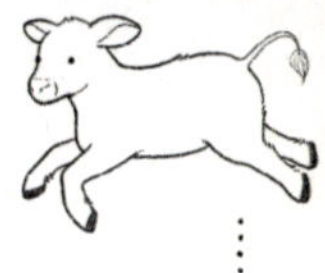

Furry Friends

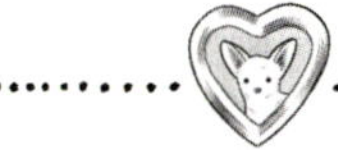

PERFECT FOR ANIMAL LOVERS!

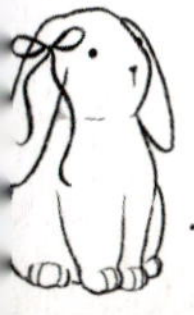 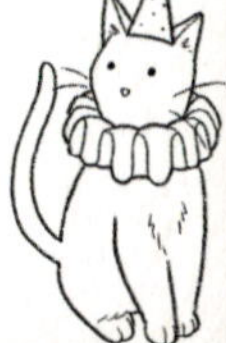

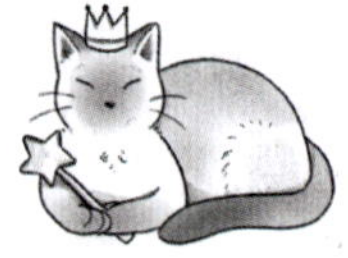

Whether you're honoring a pet with a whimsical portrait, or you want a piece that's just plain adorable, these designs are for you. Place them among other critters for a cohesive and cute feel, or surround them with flowers and plants to give them a sweet home.

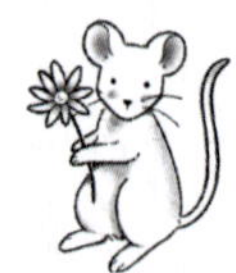

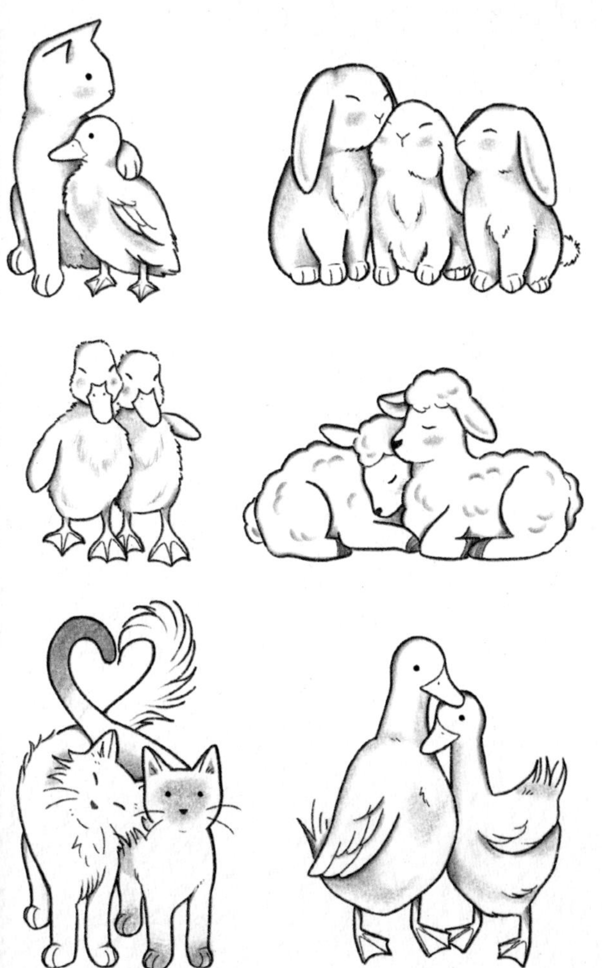

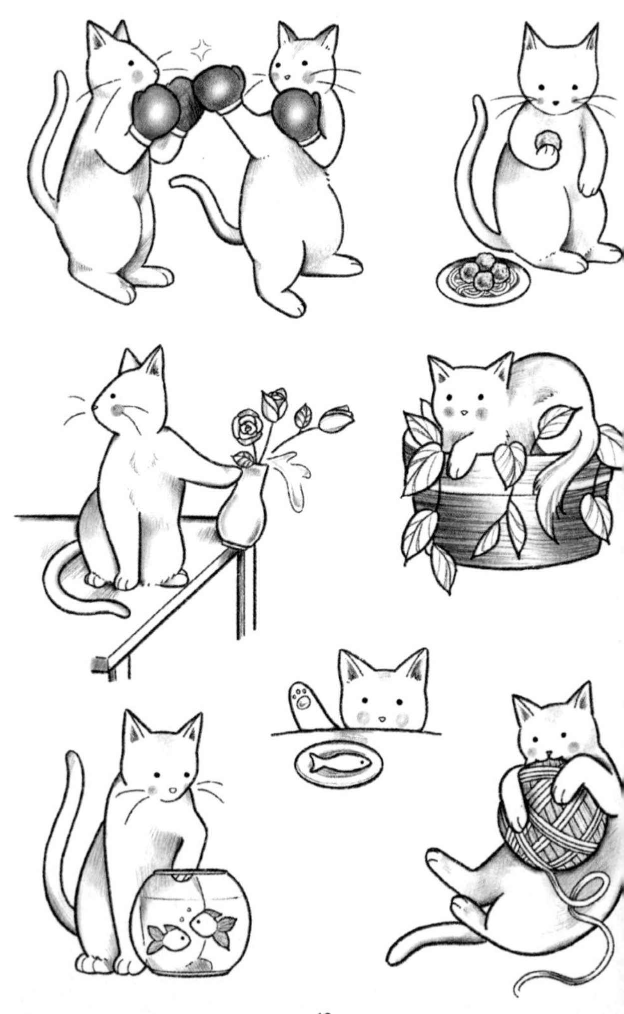

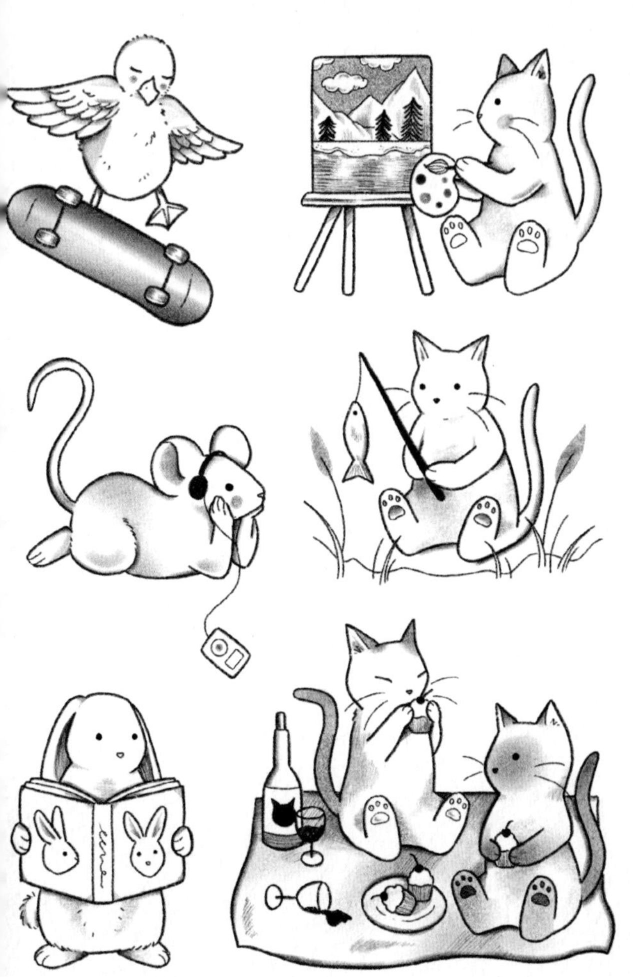

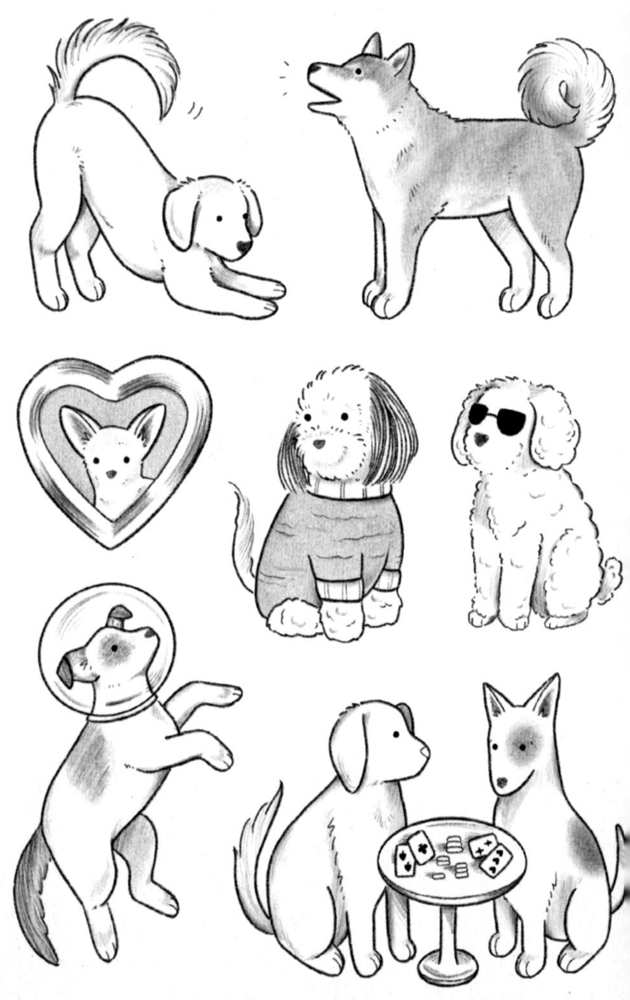

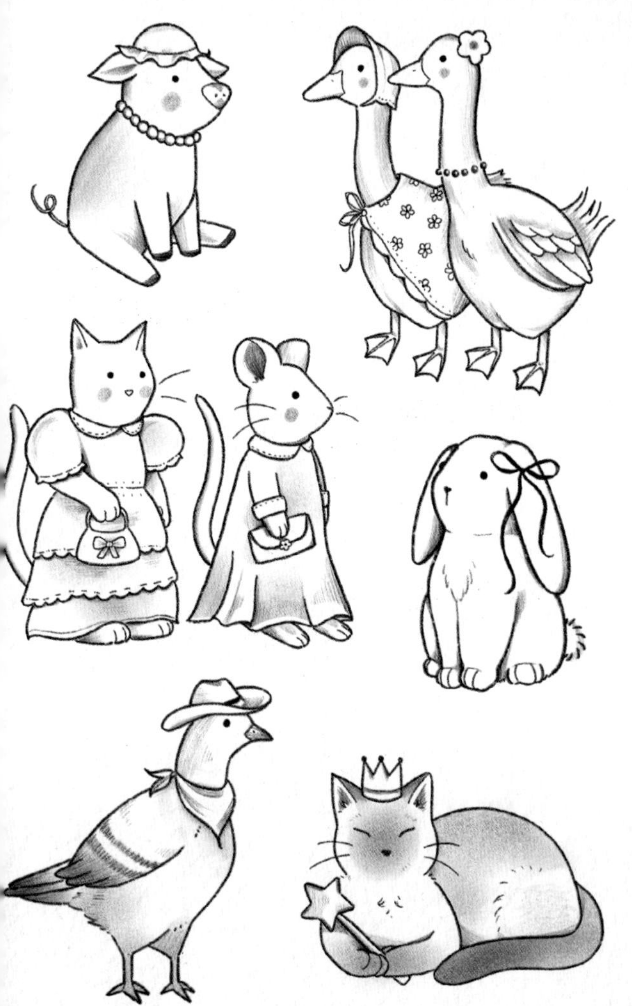

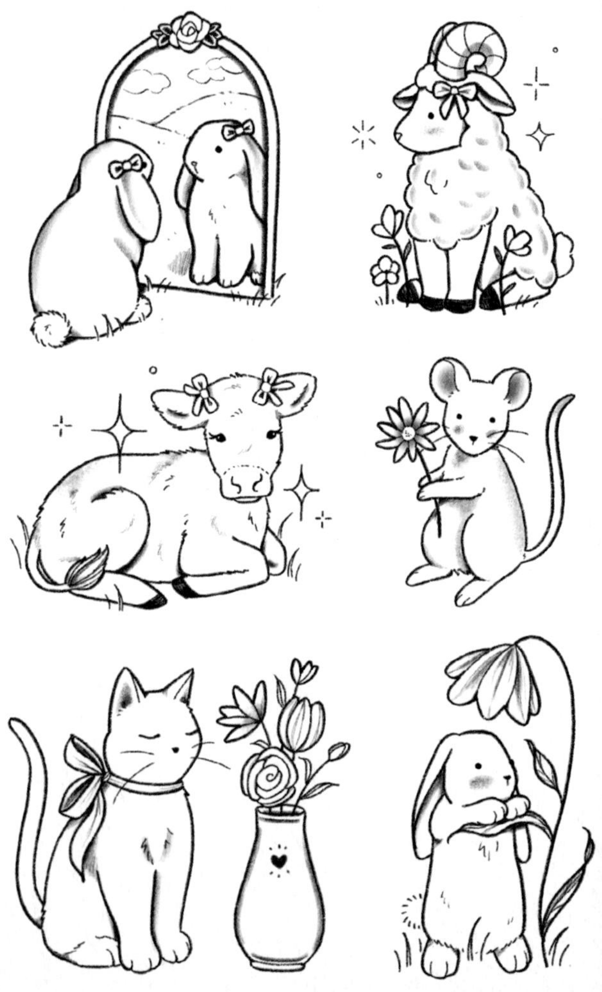

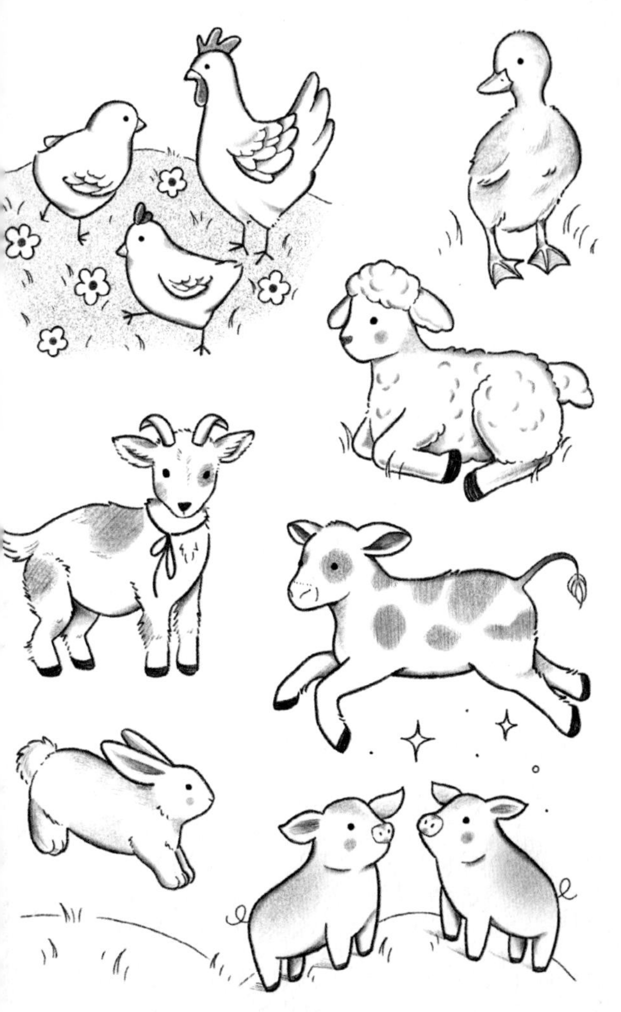

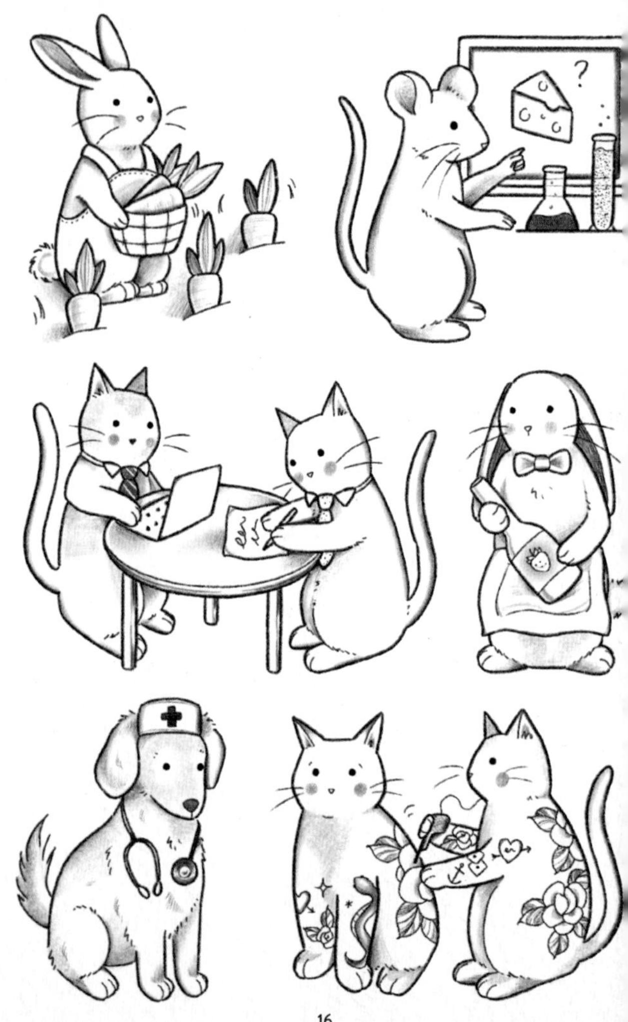

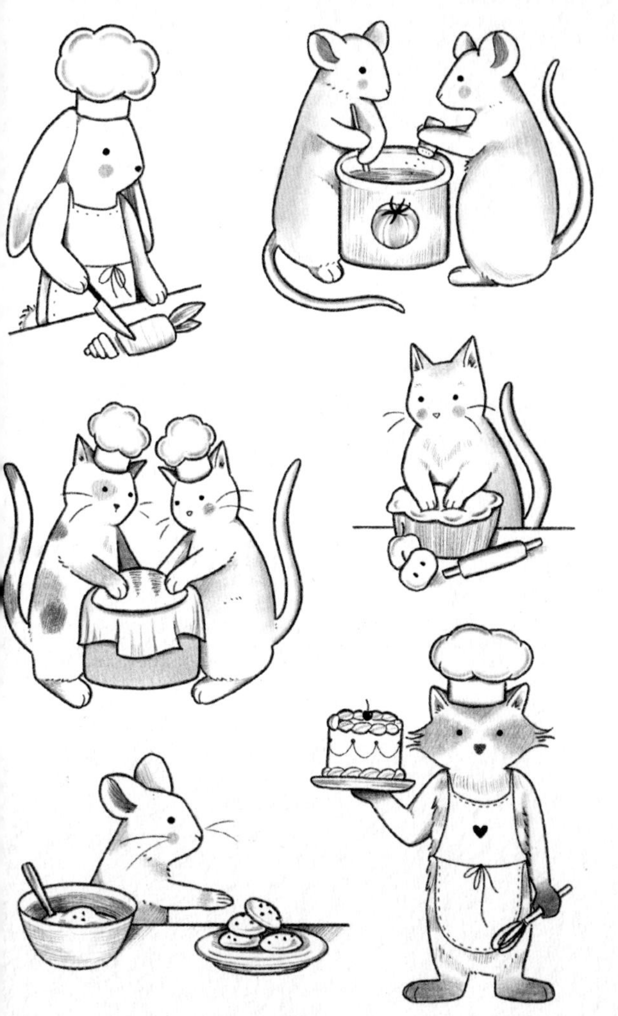

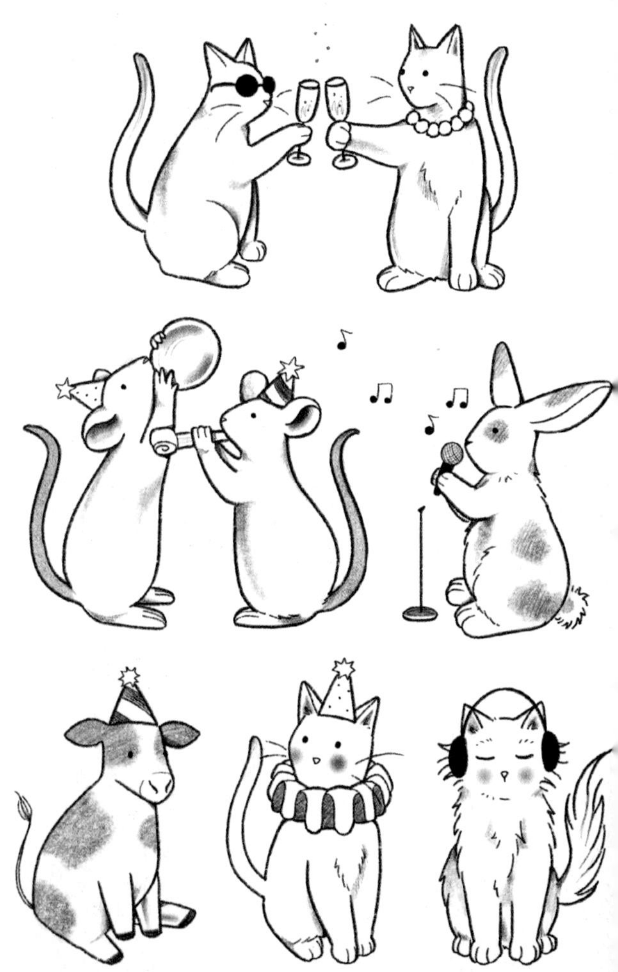

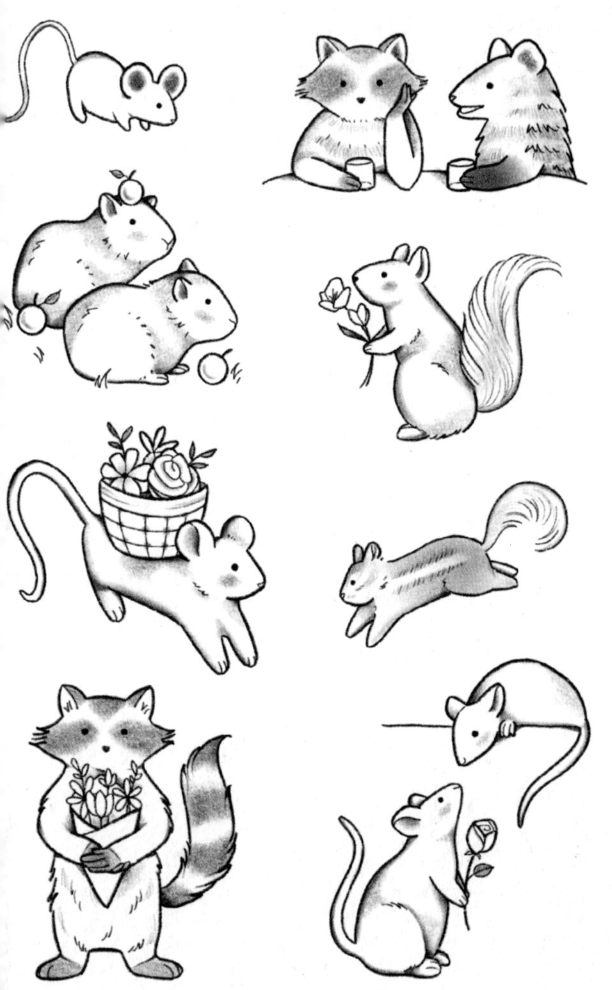

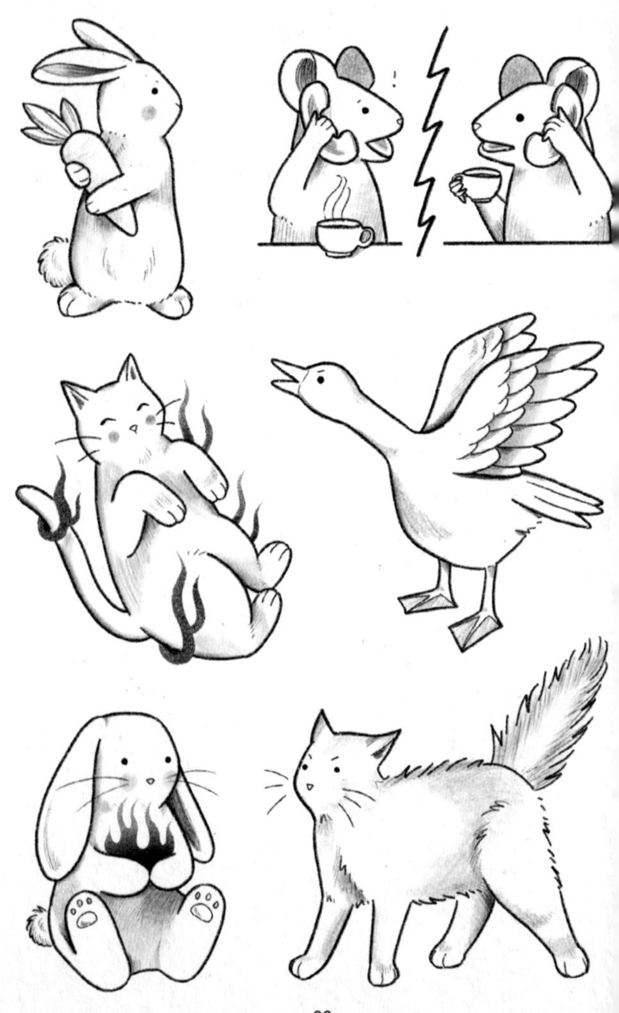

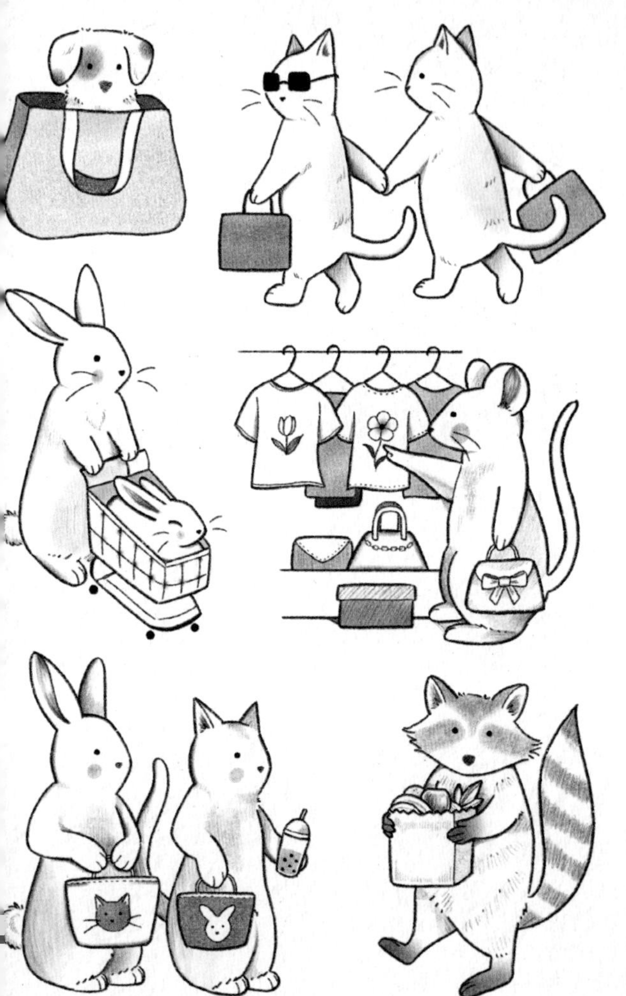

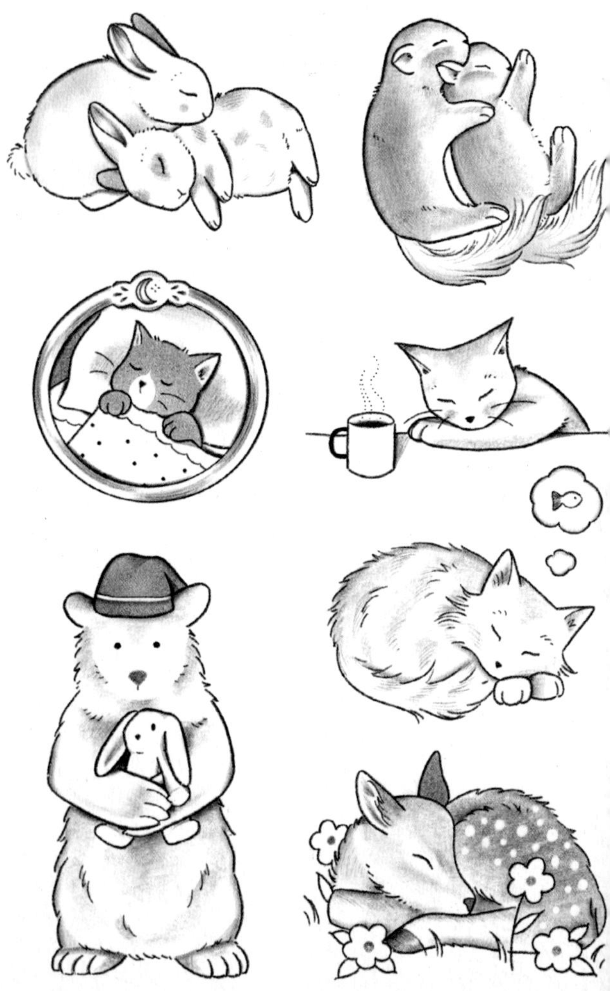

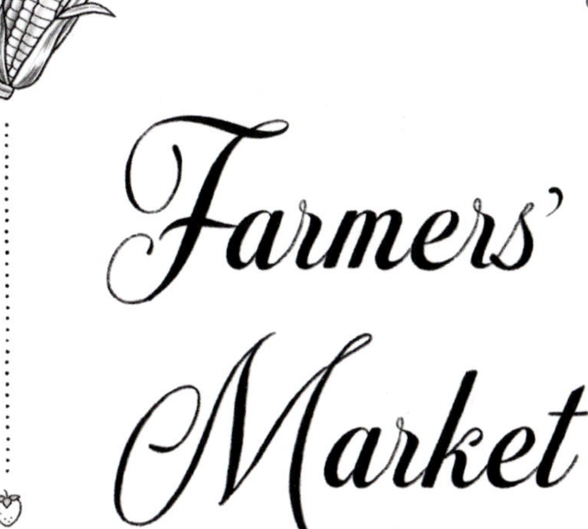

Farmers' Market

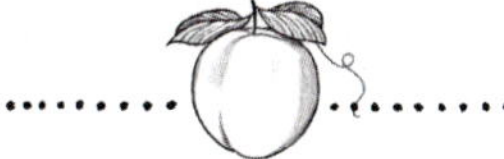

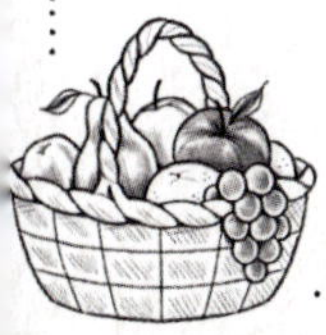

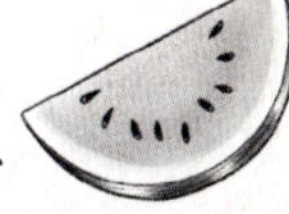

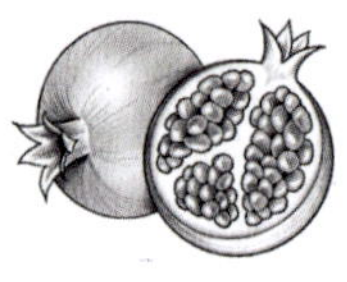

Try a fruit that reminds you of a
place you love, a vegetable that
grows in your garden, or a basket
full of your favorites! Add leaves
and flowers for more movement,
or arrange a unique still life for
a sticker sleeve look.

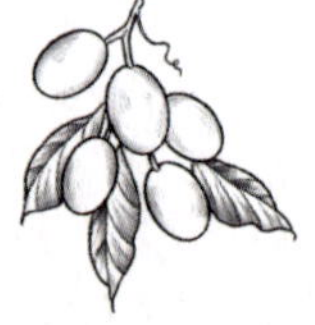

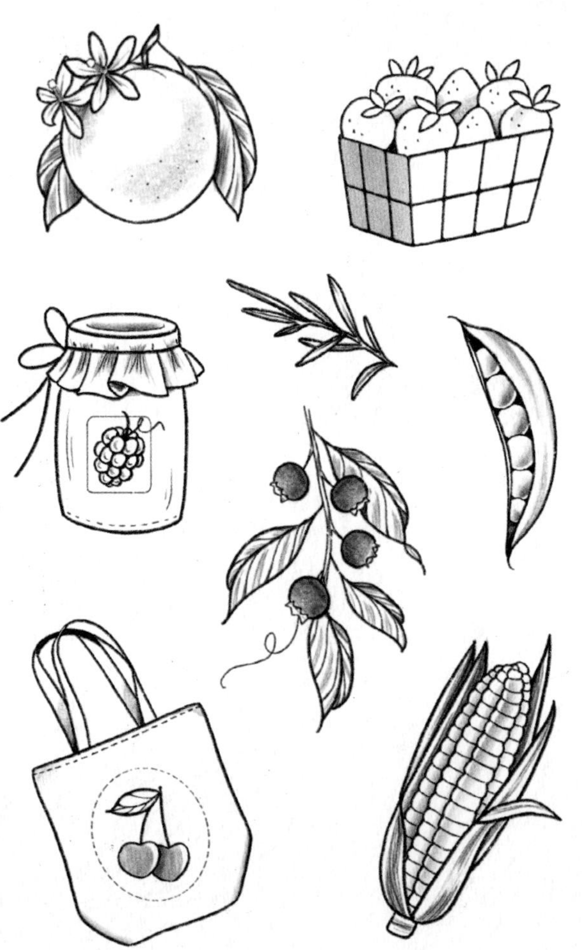

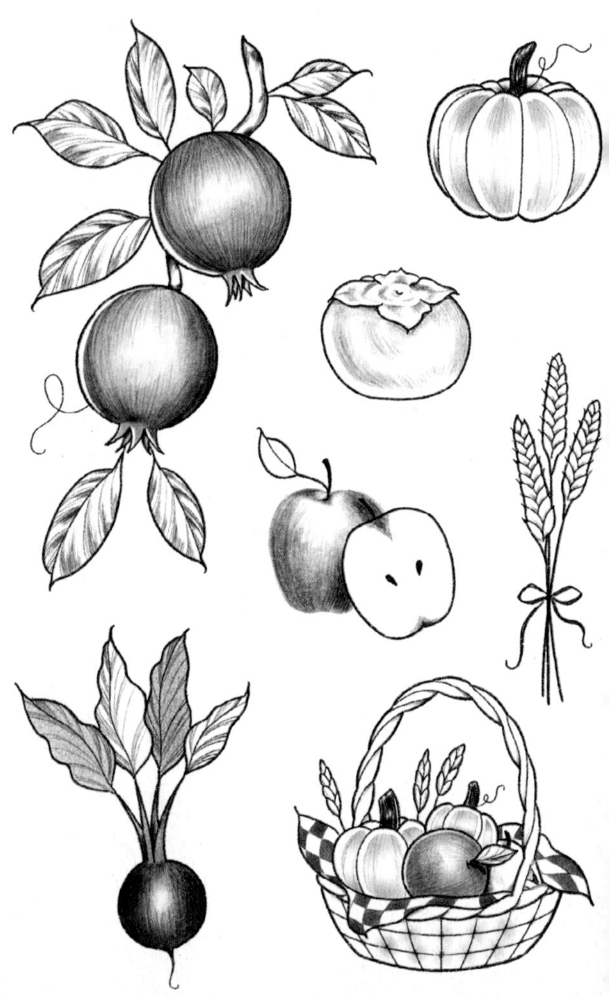

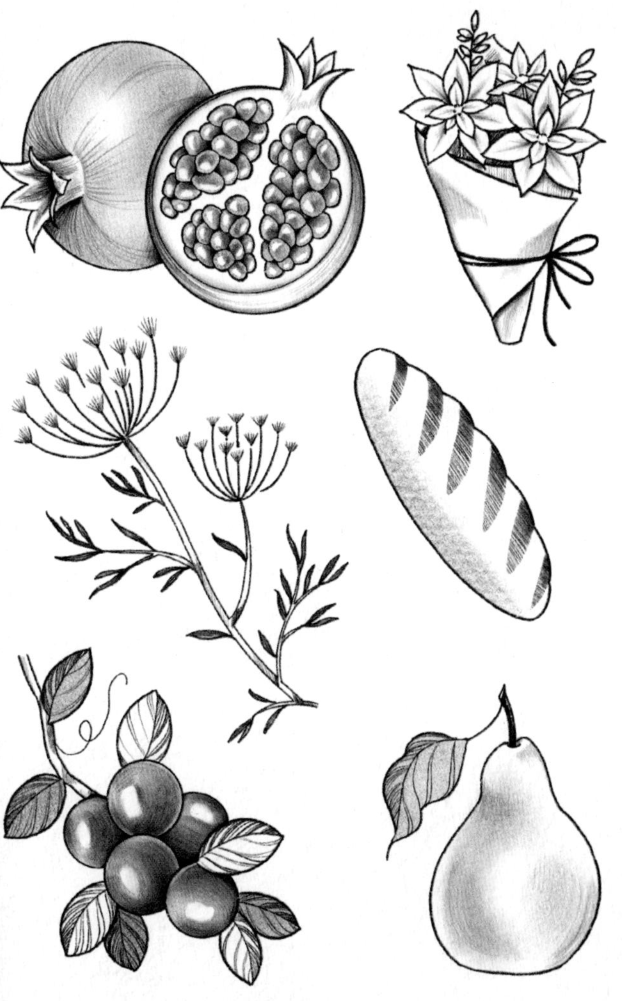

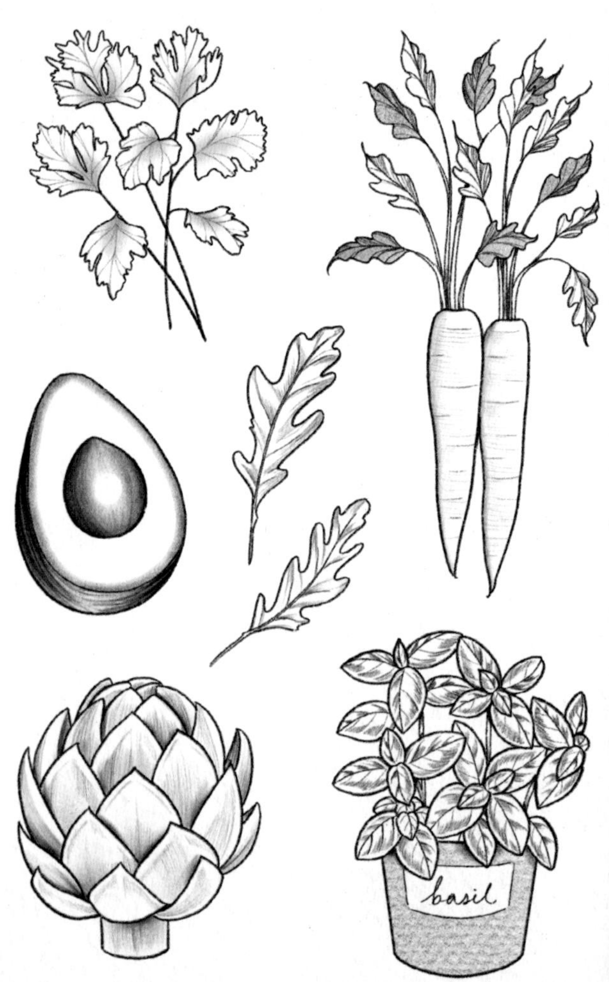
basil

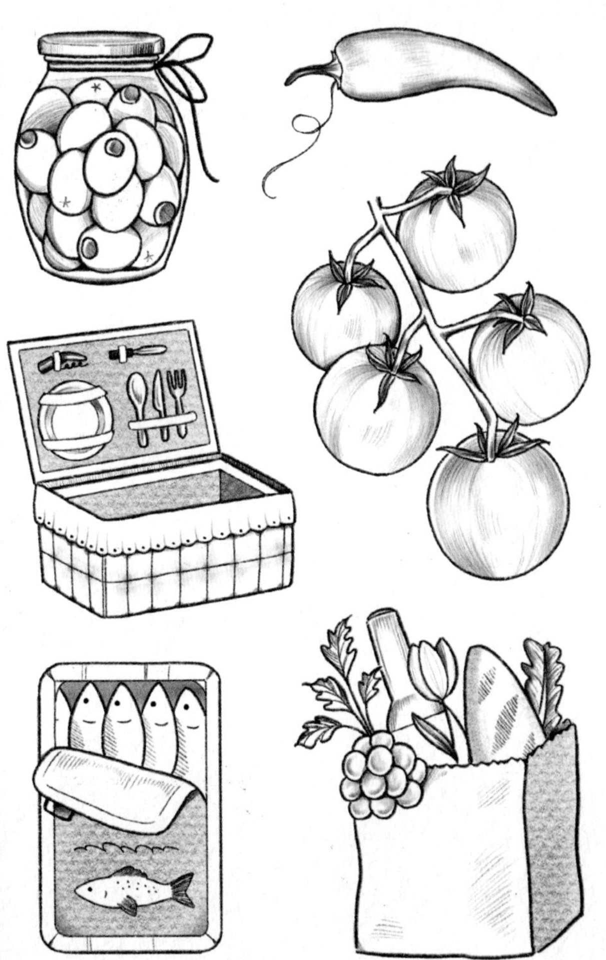

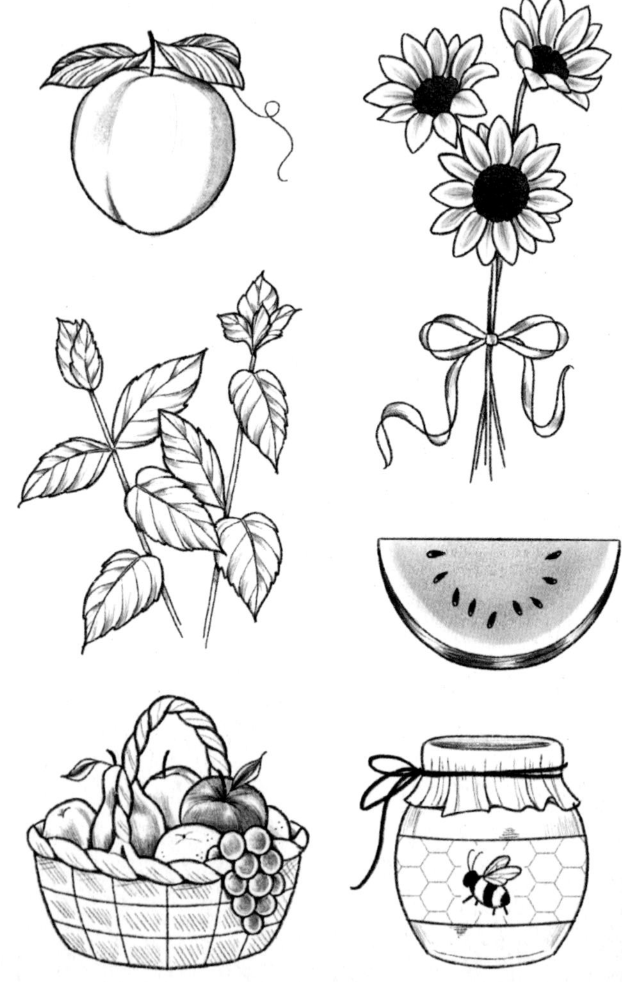

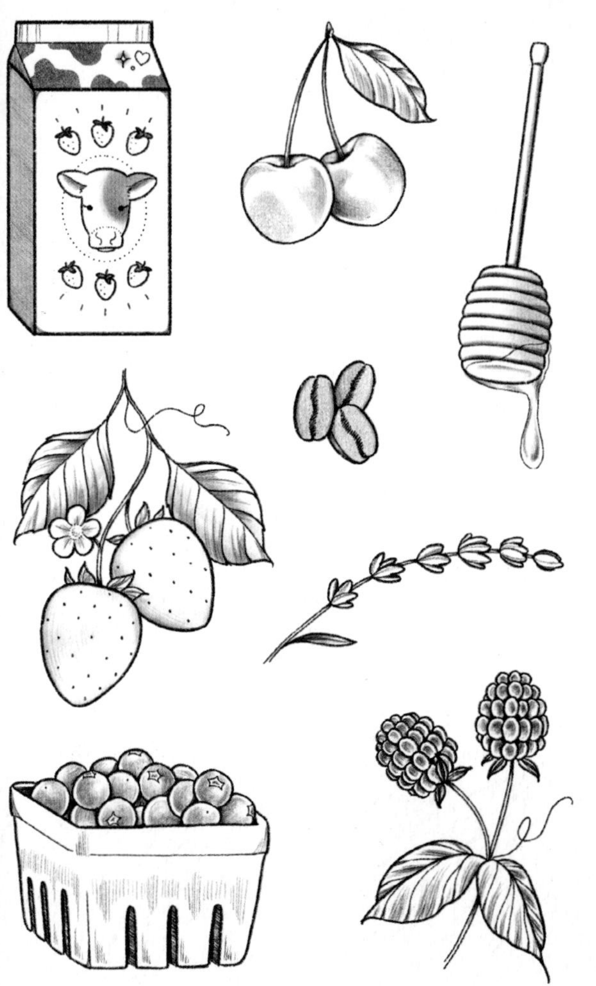

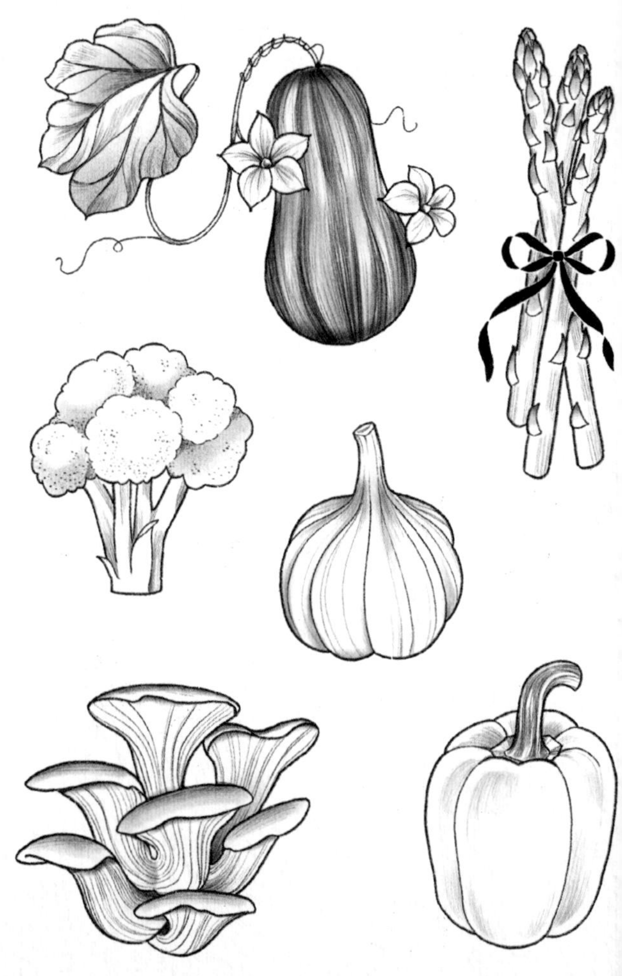

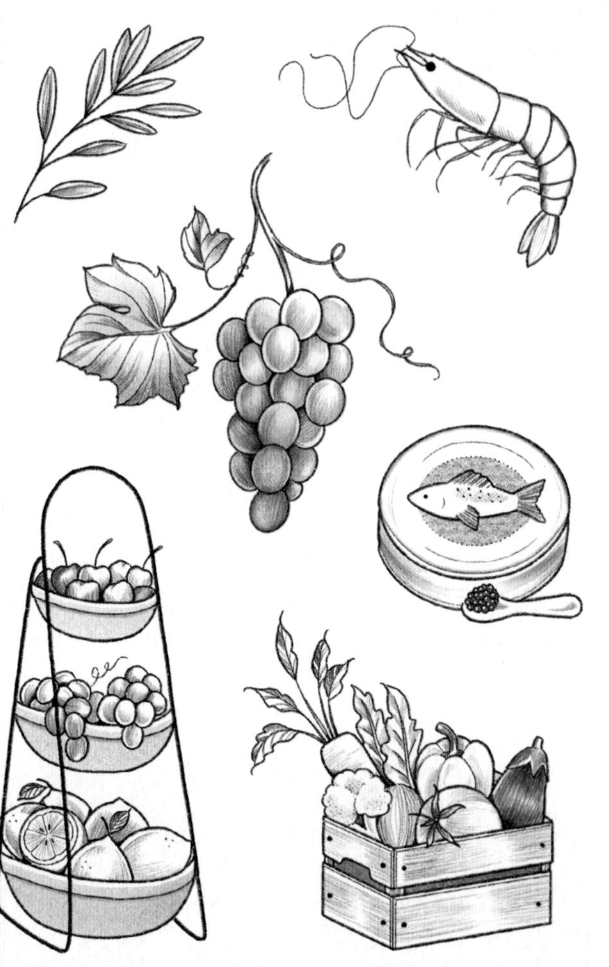

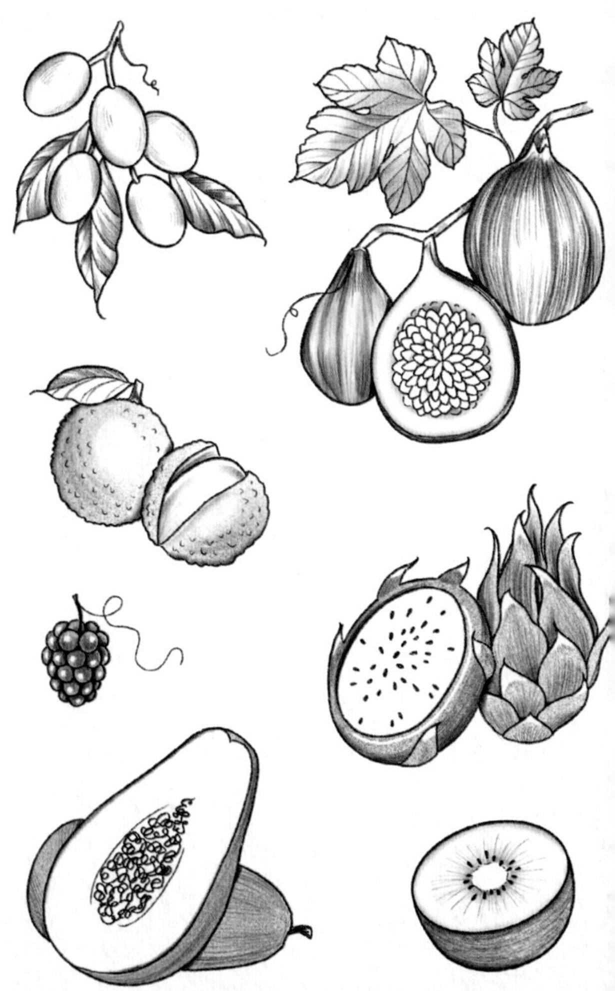

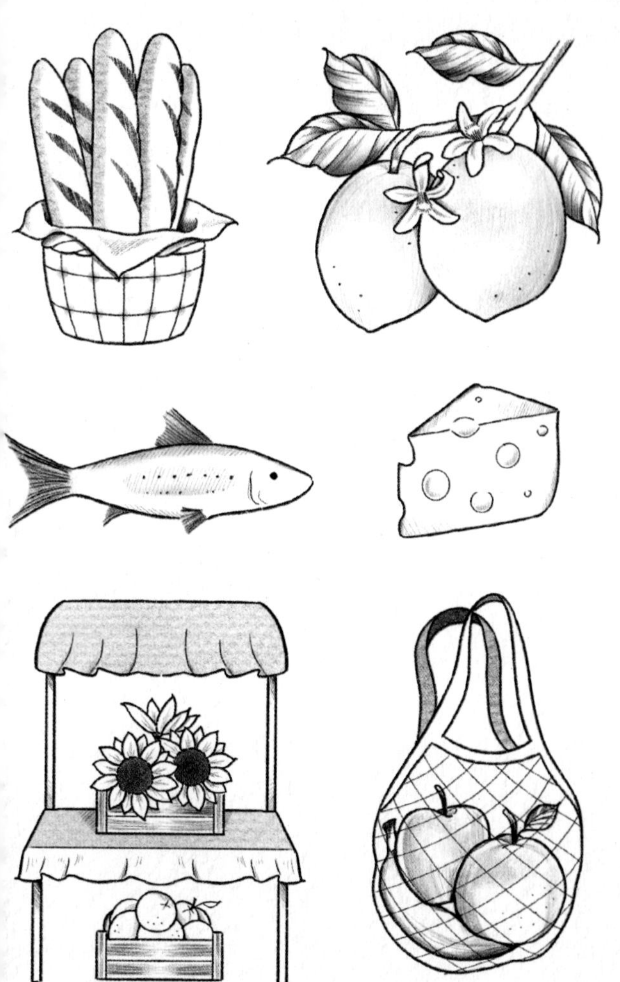

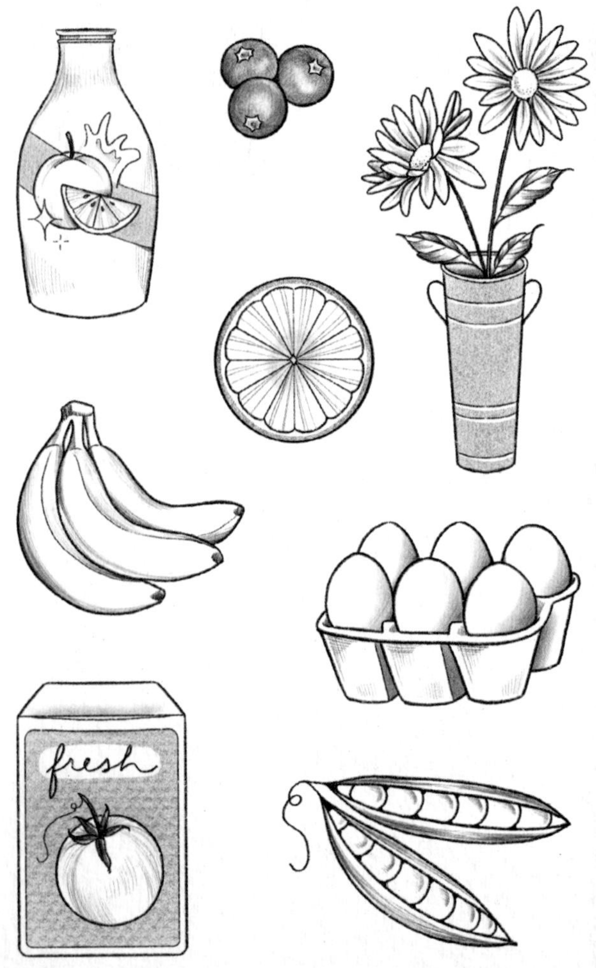
fresh

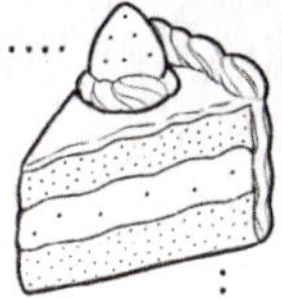

Sweet Treats

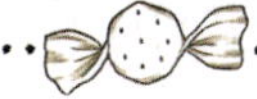

A COLLECTION OF DESSERTS AND
SNACKS FOR THOSE WHO APPRECIATE
THE SWEETER THINGS IN LIFE.

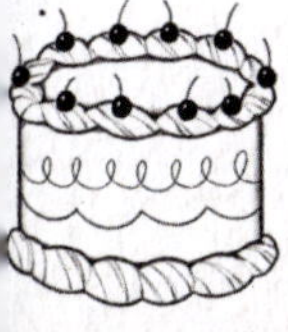
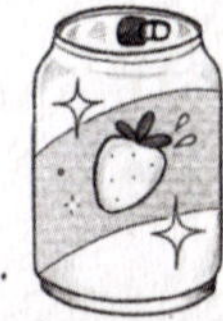

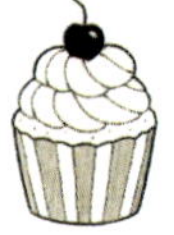

Be inspired by pies that remind you

of family gatherings, cakes from

special occasions, or candies that

always satisfy your sweet tooth.

A tasty way to fill the gaps

in your sleeve!

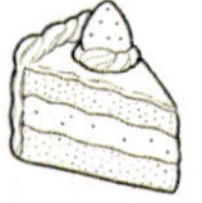

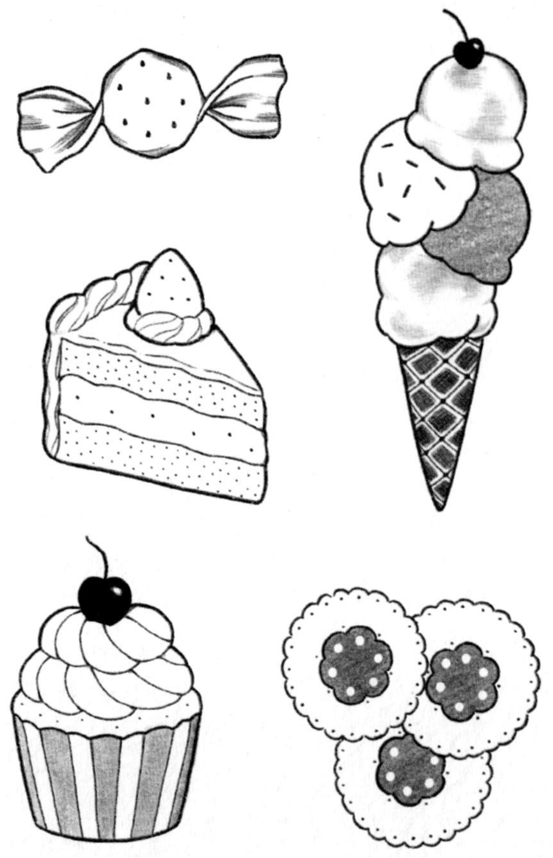

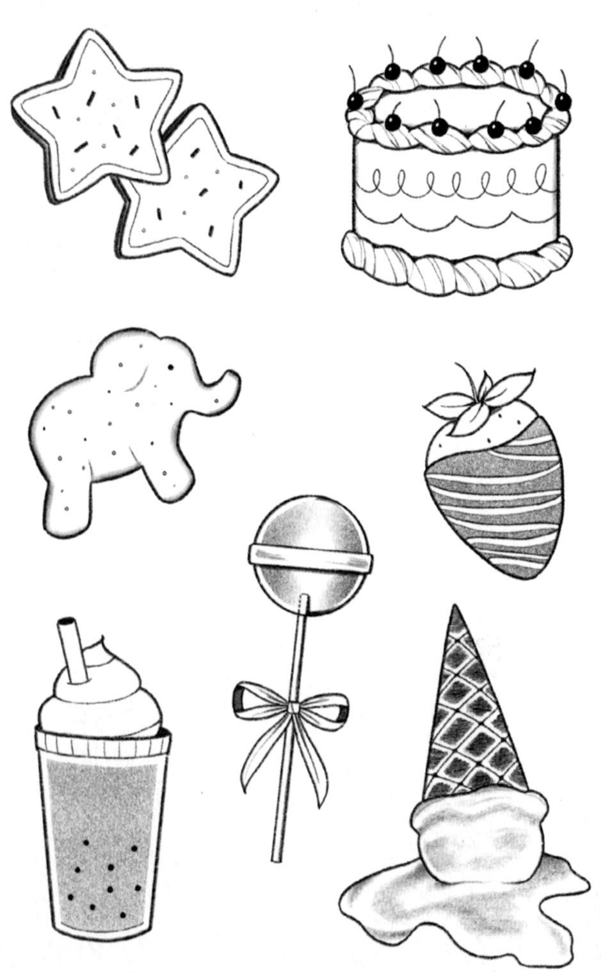

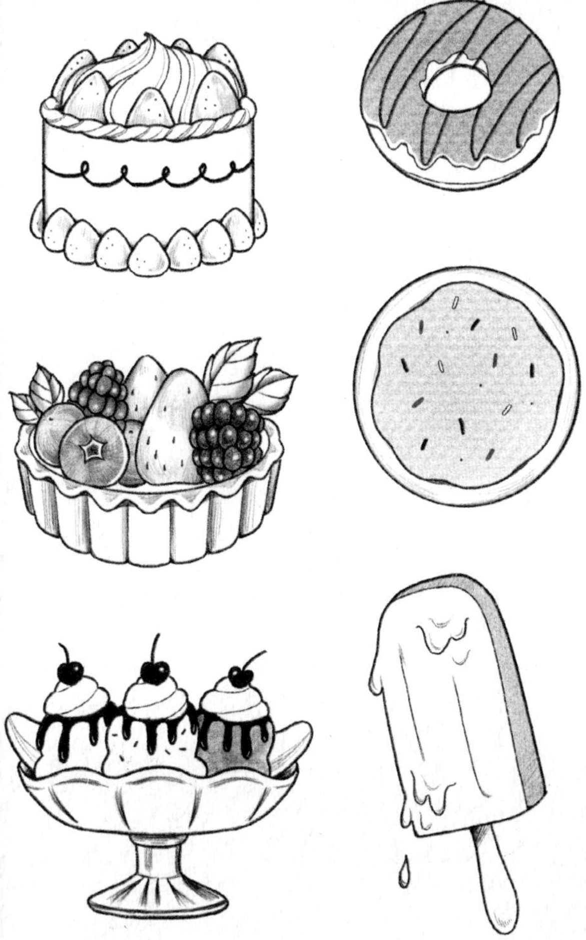

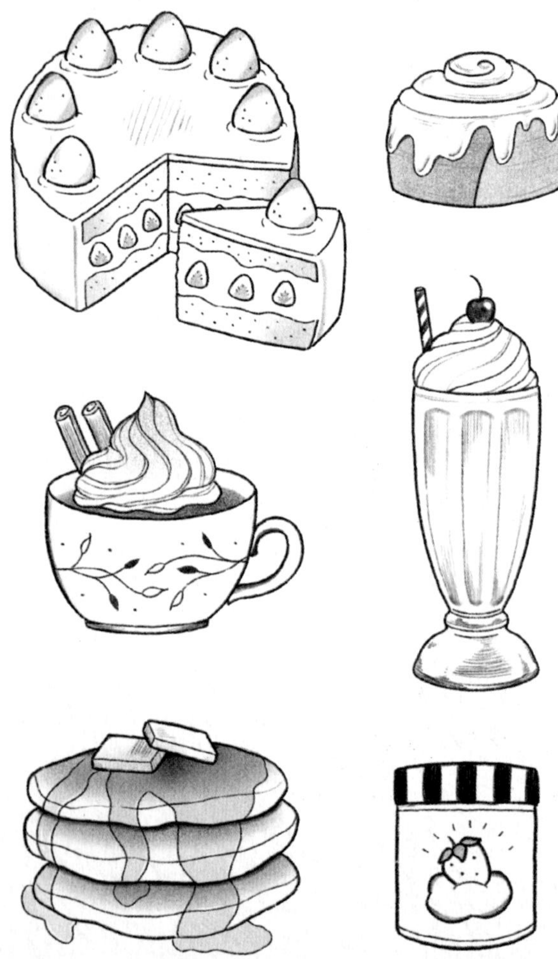

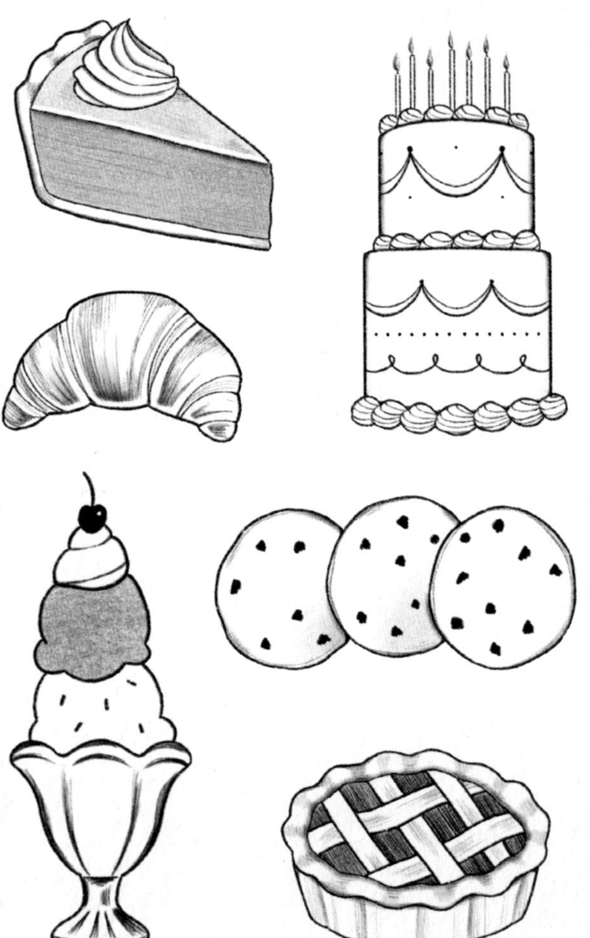

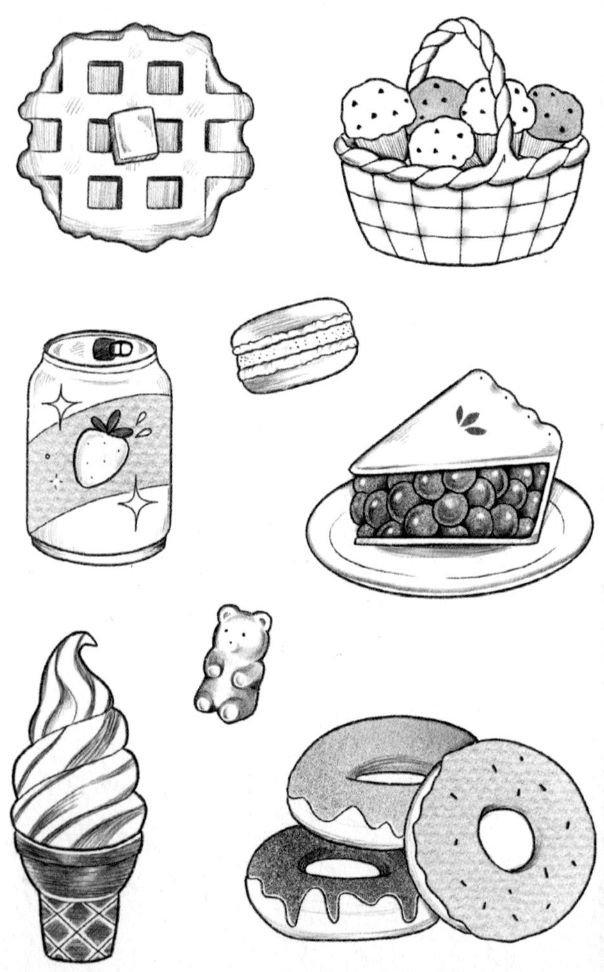

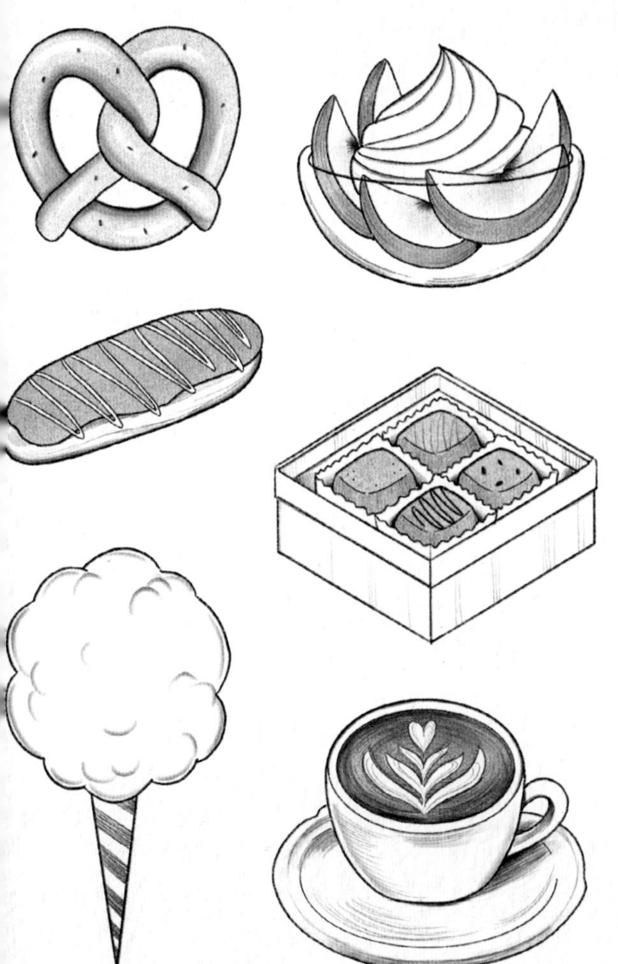

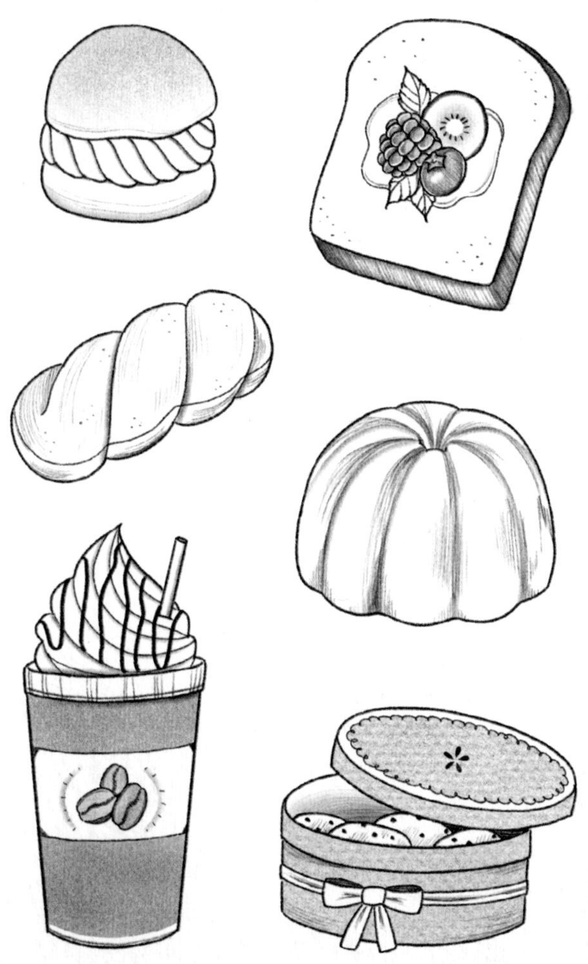

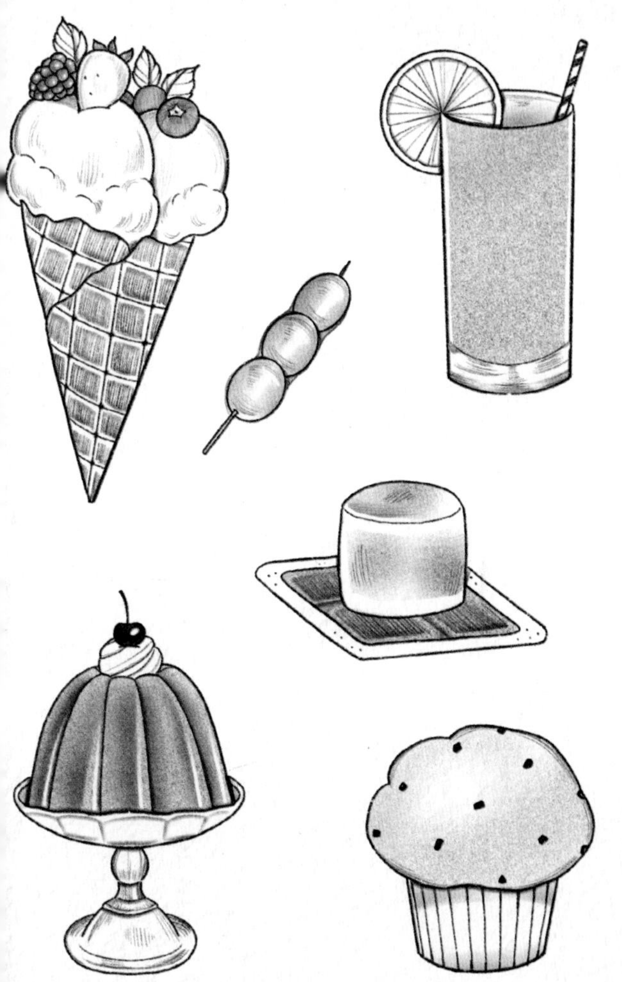

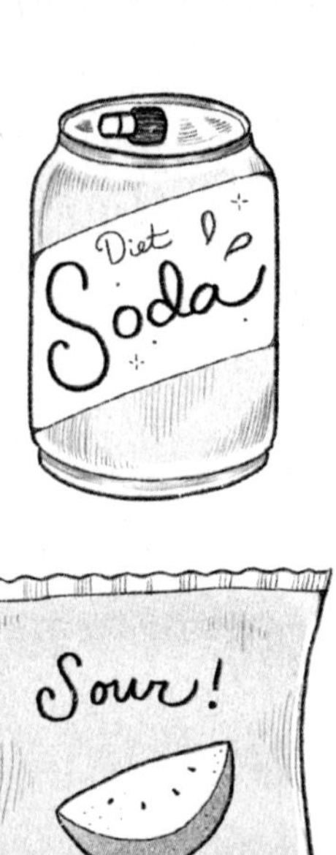
Diet
Soda

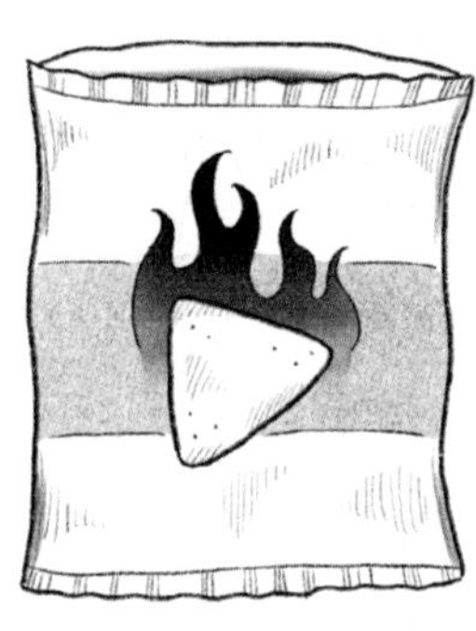

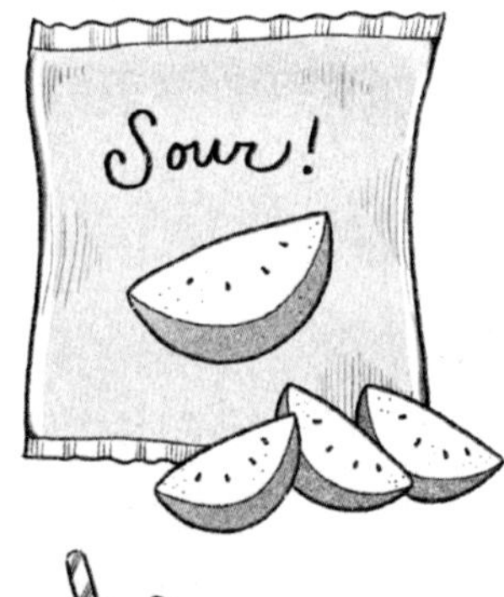
Sour!

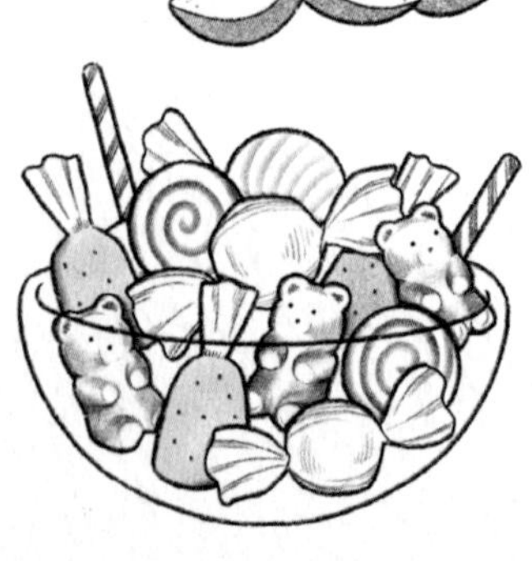

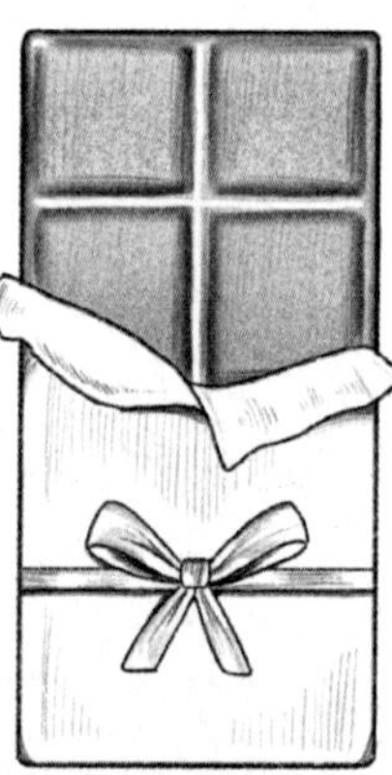

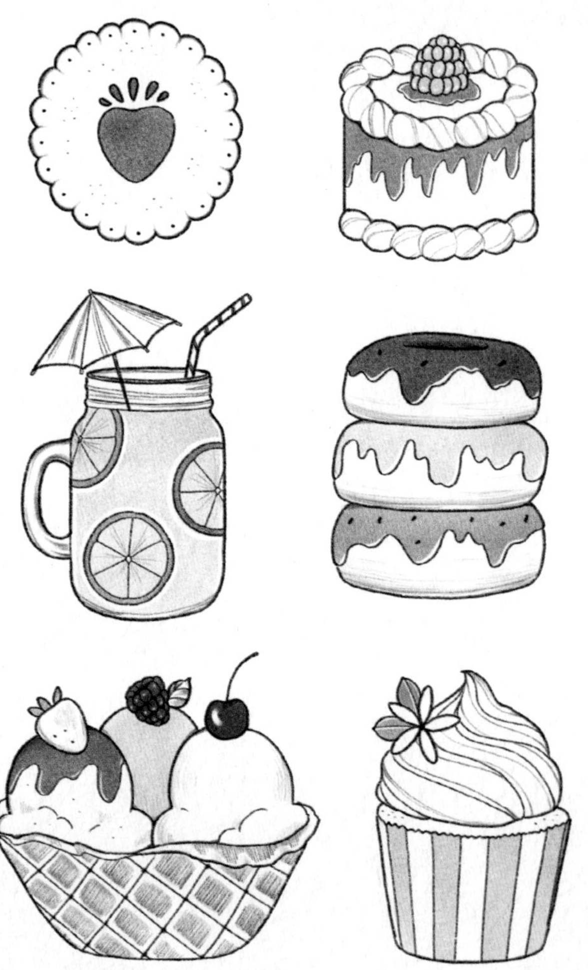

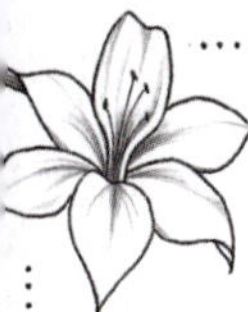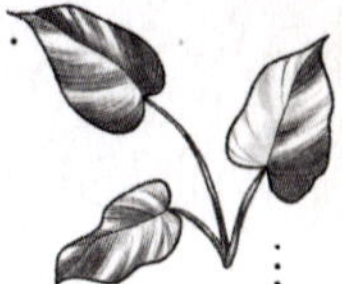

Garden
Paradise

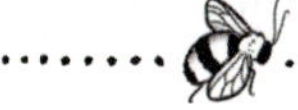

DREAMY BOTANICAL VIBES
FOR PLANT AND FLOWER
LOVERS ALIKE.

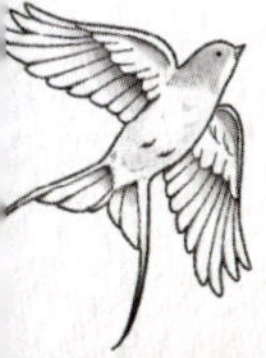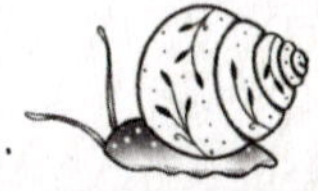

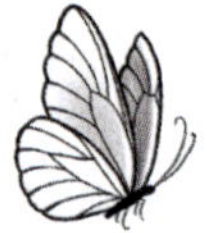

Create an ethereal scene with sweet
cherubs, build a bouquet of birth
flowers, or adopt a houseplant you'll
never need to water. These designs
are great for bendy spots like elbows,
knees, and shoulders—leaves and
petals flow nicely everywhere!

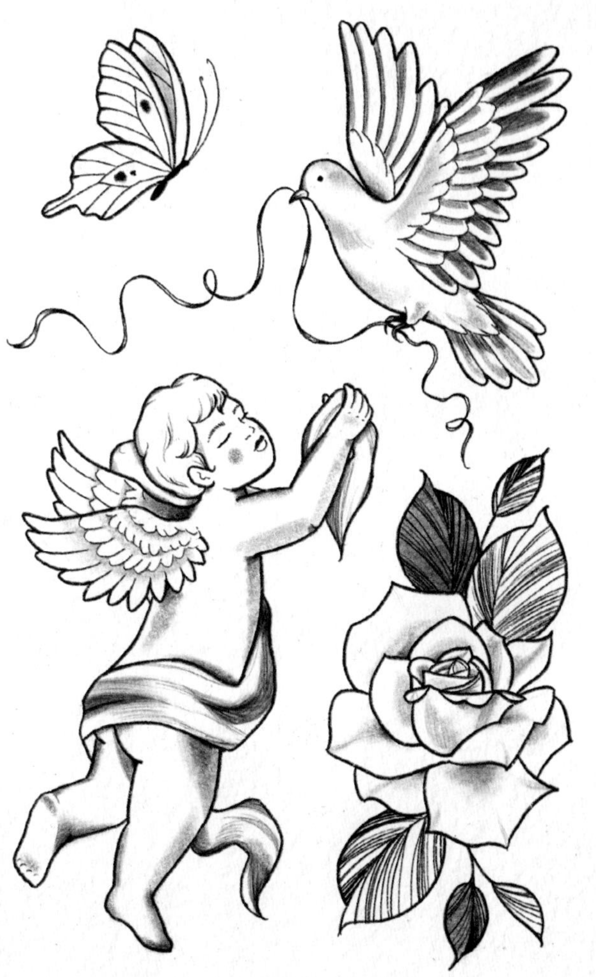

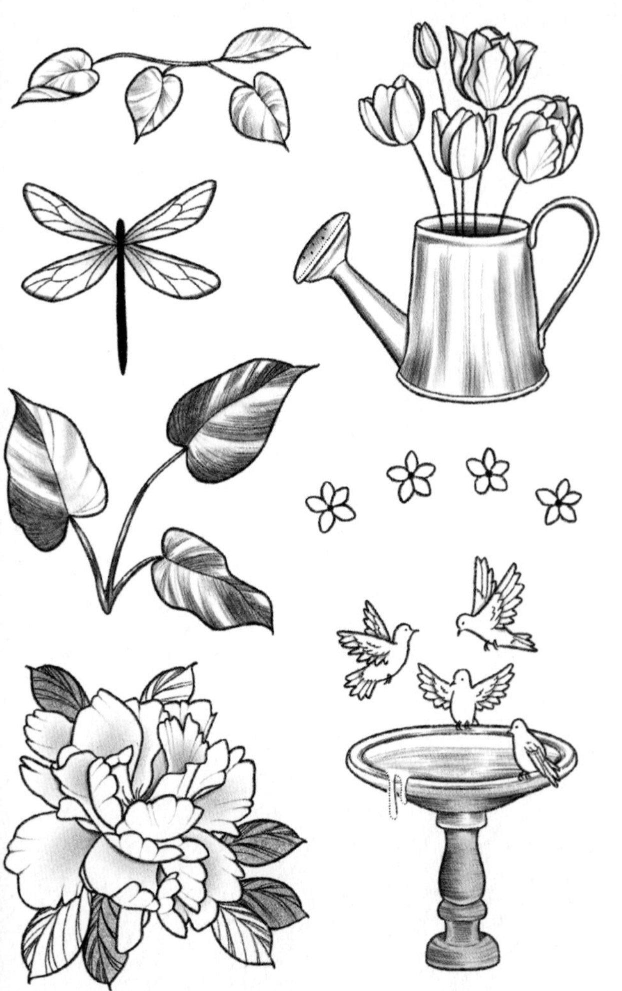

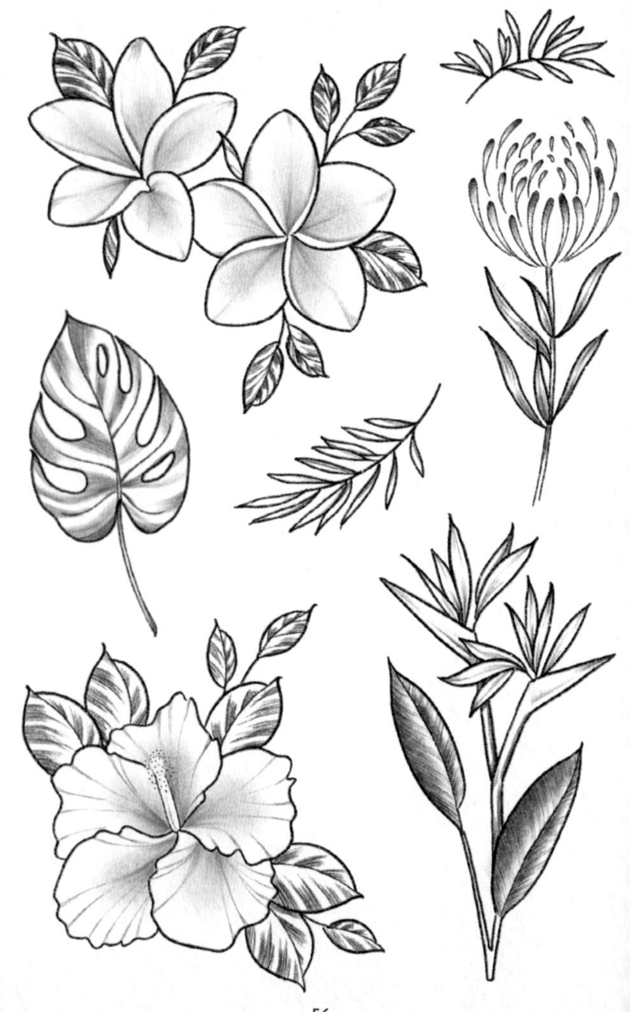

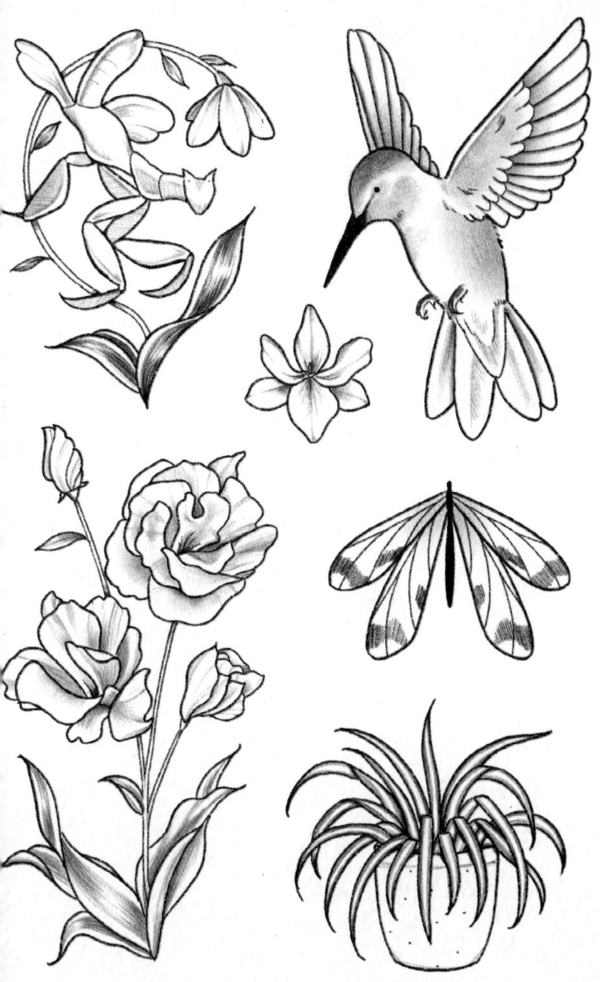

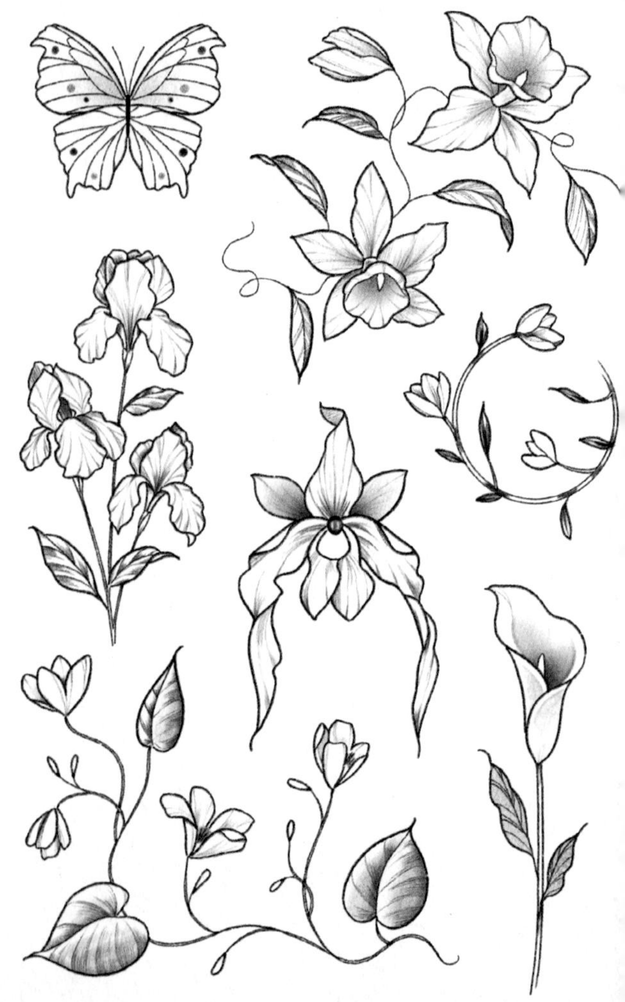

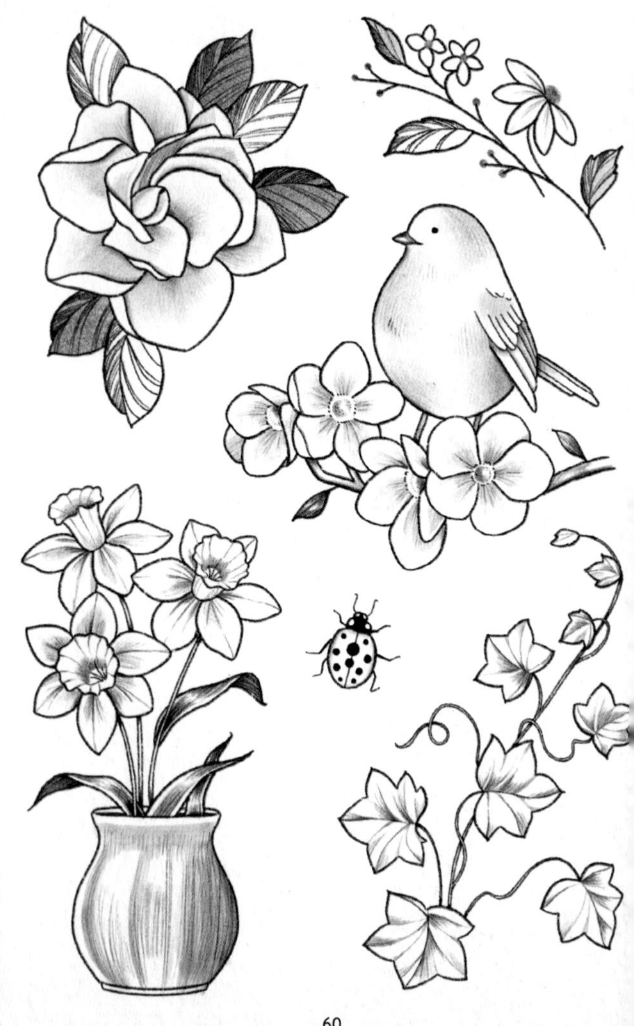

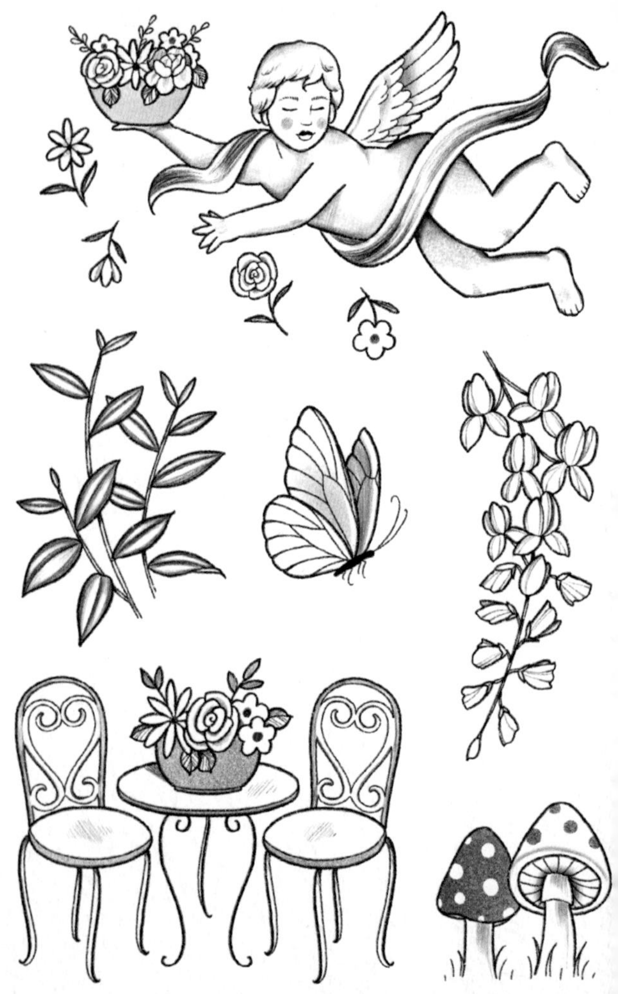

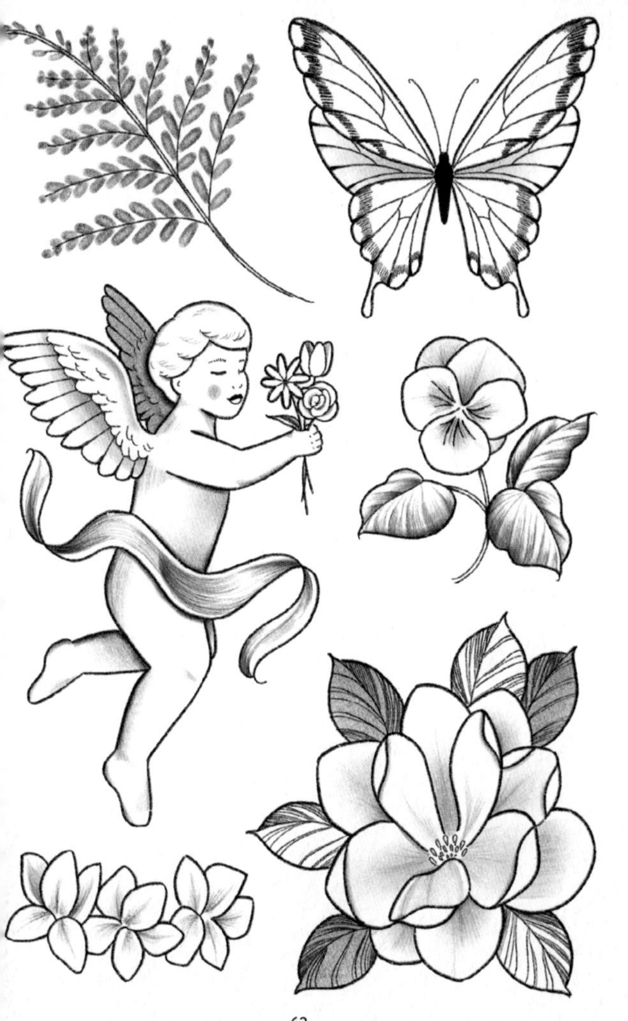

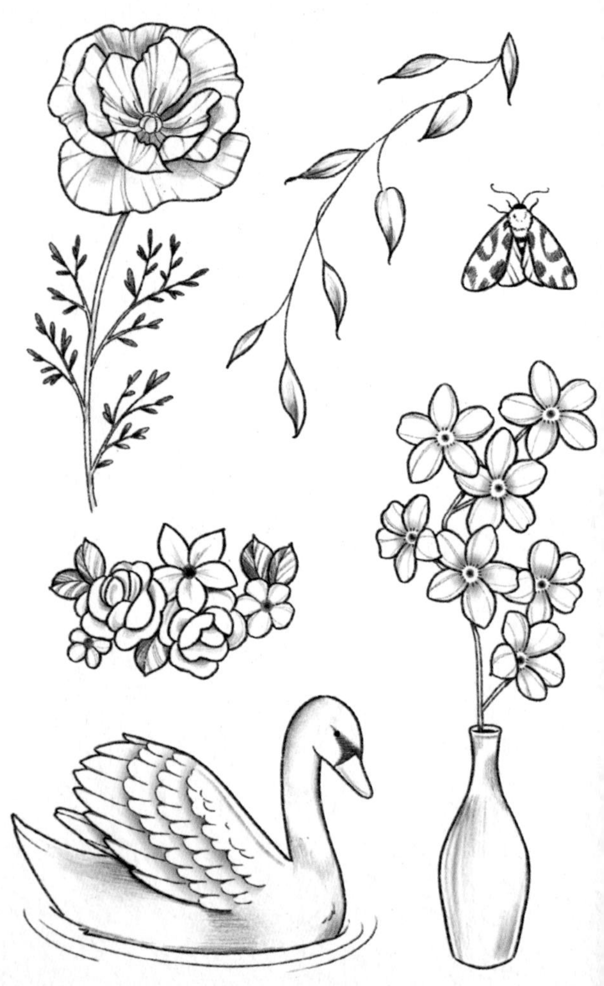

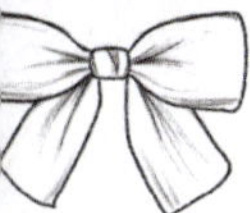
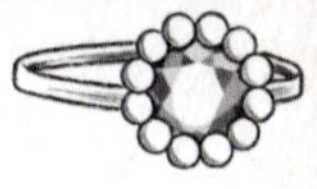

Jewelry Box

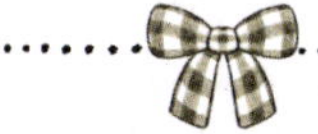

PERMANENT ACCESSORIES
TO GO WITH EVERY OUTFIT!

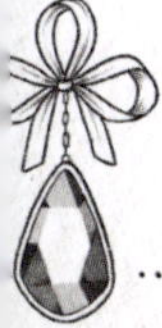

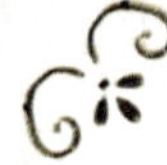

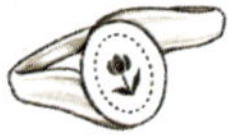

Decorate with a sentimental piece
of jewelry, get a matching locket
with your bestie, or weave a ribbon
around other tattoos. Itty bitty
adornments look especially elegant
with wrist and ankle placements.

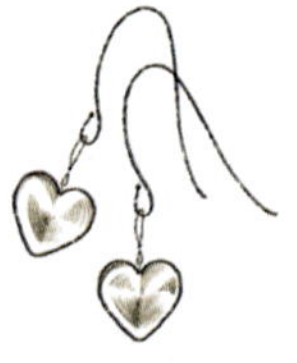

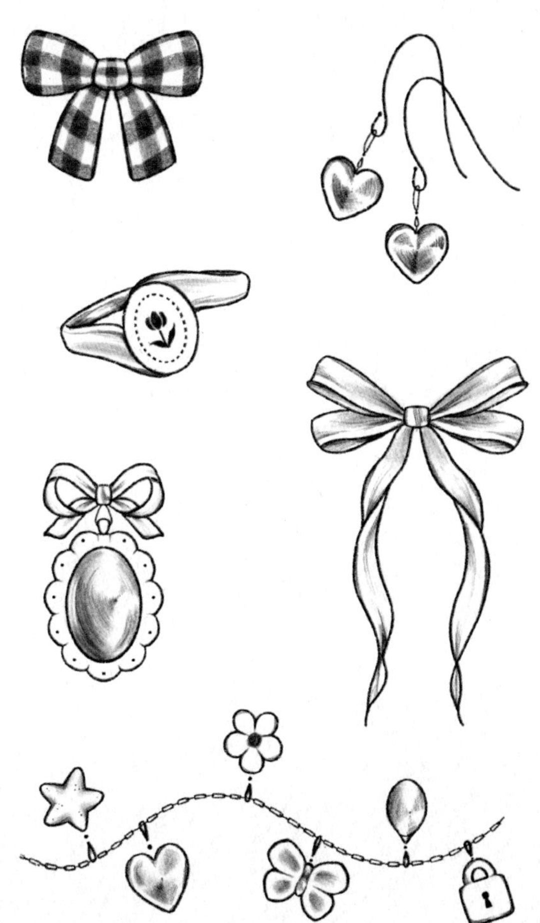

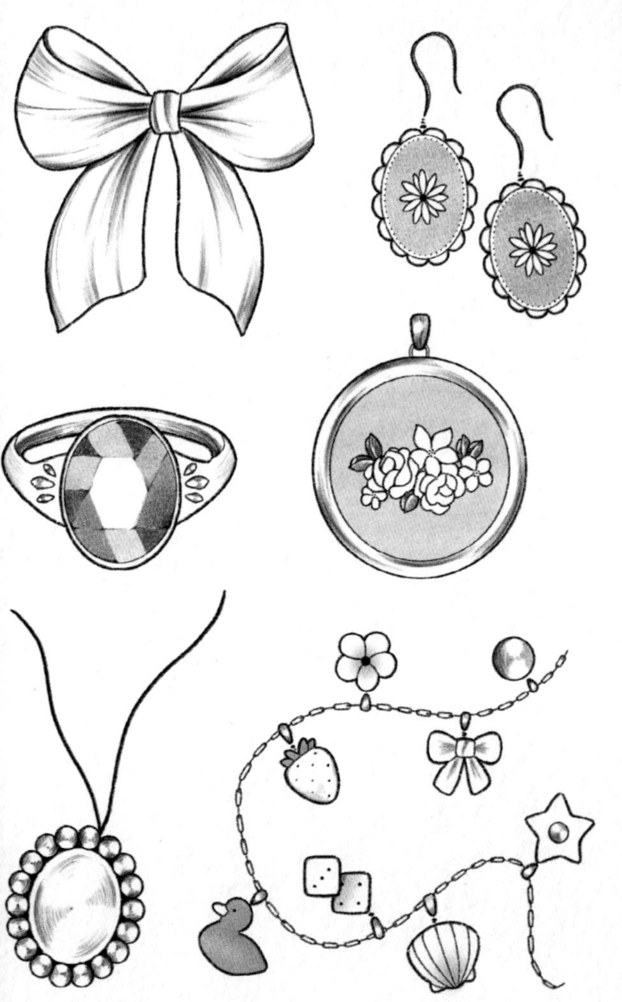

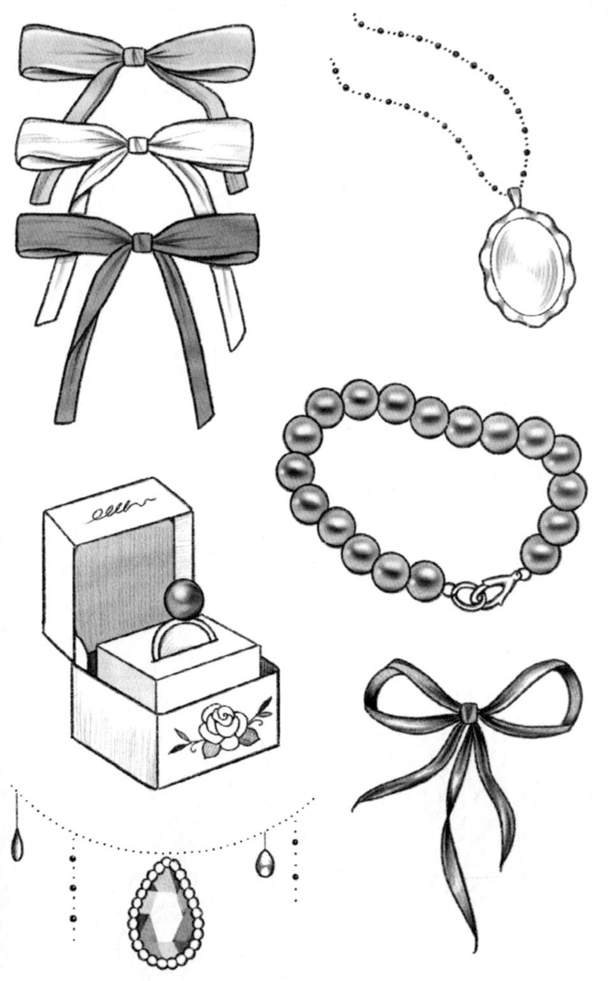

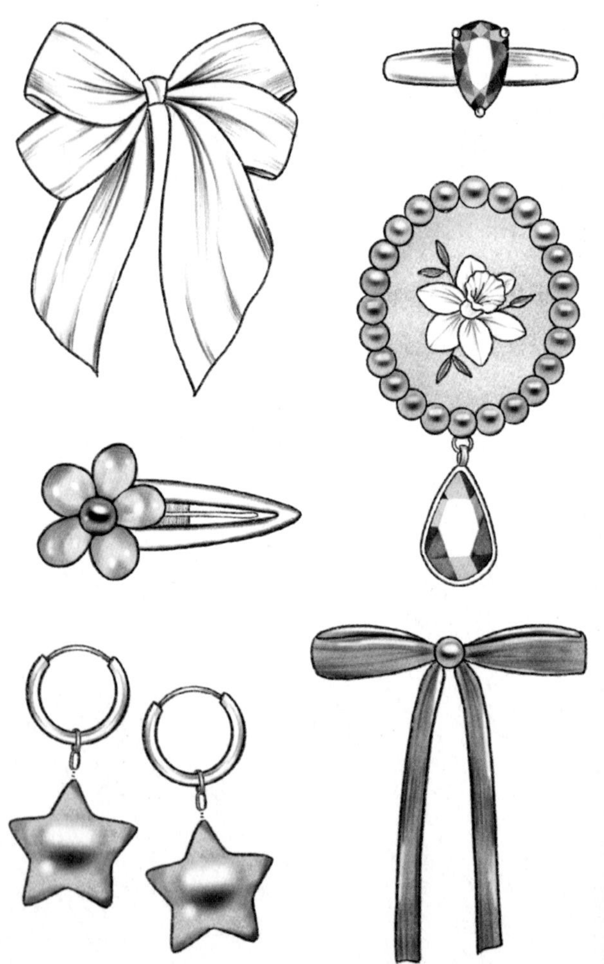

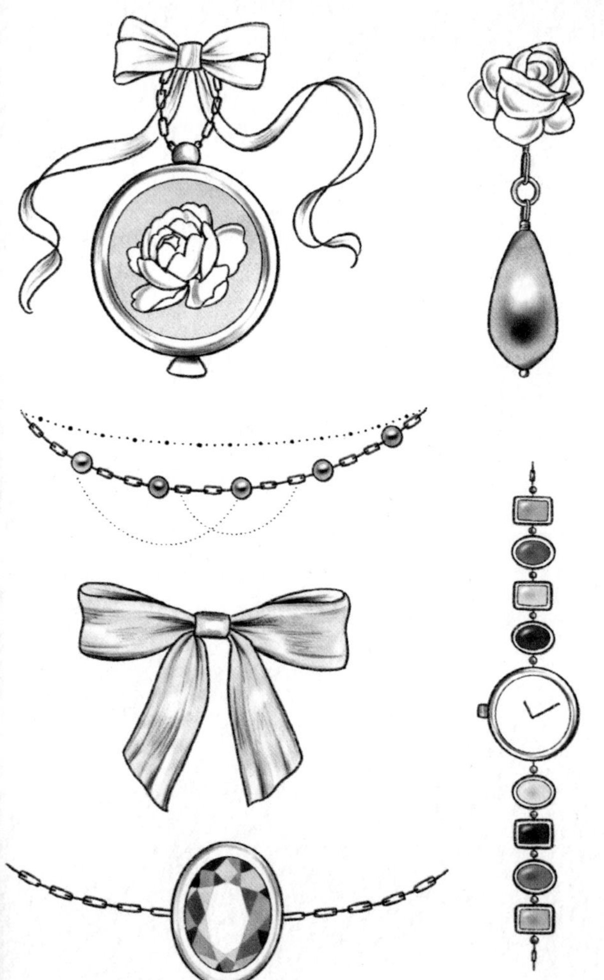

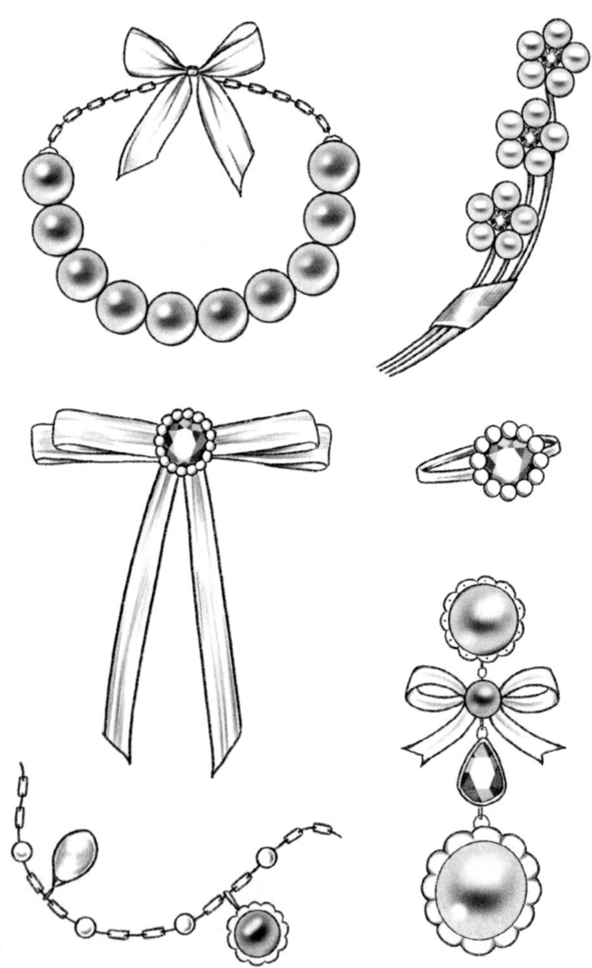

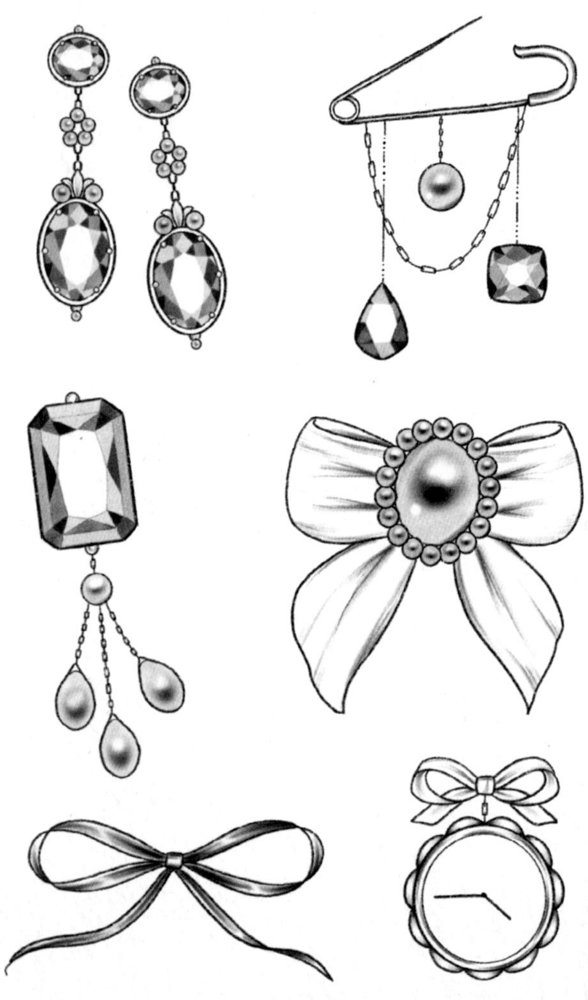

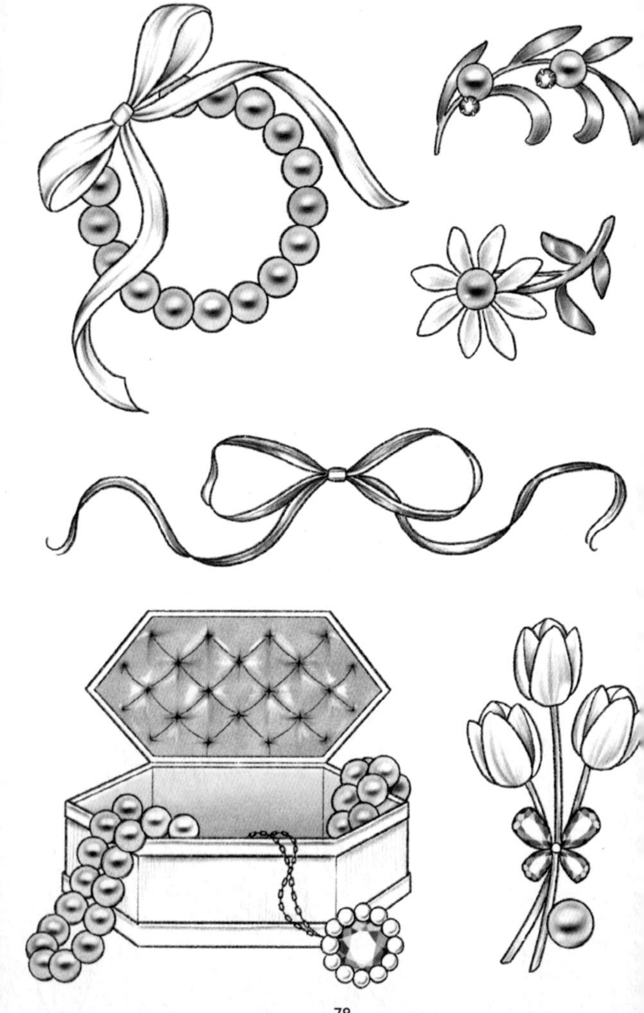

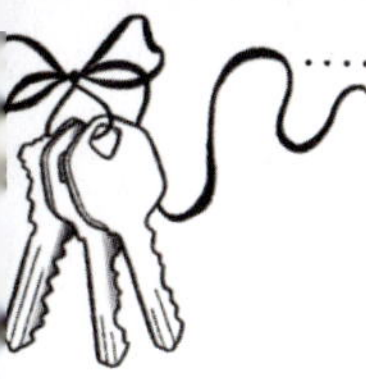
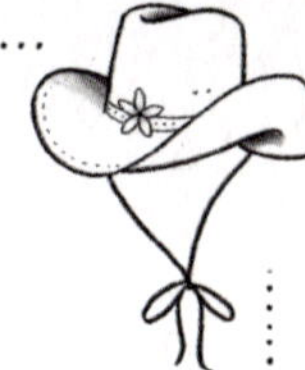

This & That

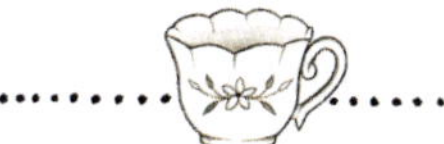

A BEAUTIFUL HODGEPODGE
OF THEMES.

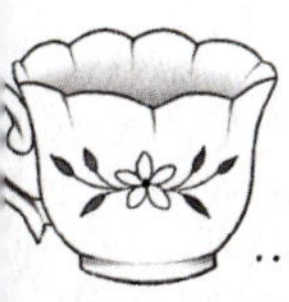
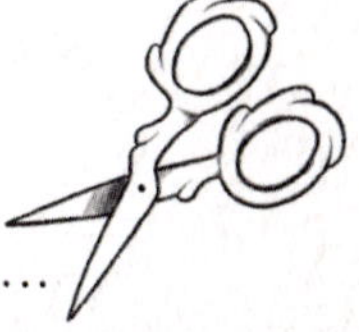

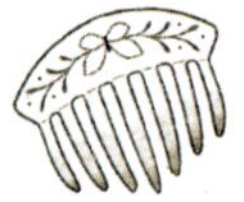

Let the trinkets on your shelf inspire

you, and add a unique stamp, a

vintage key, or a cowboy boot

to your tattoo collection—

the possibilities are endless!

Perfect for a sticker sleeve look.

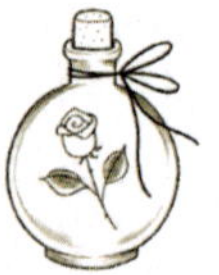

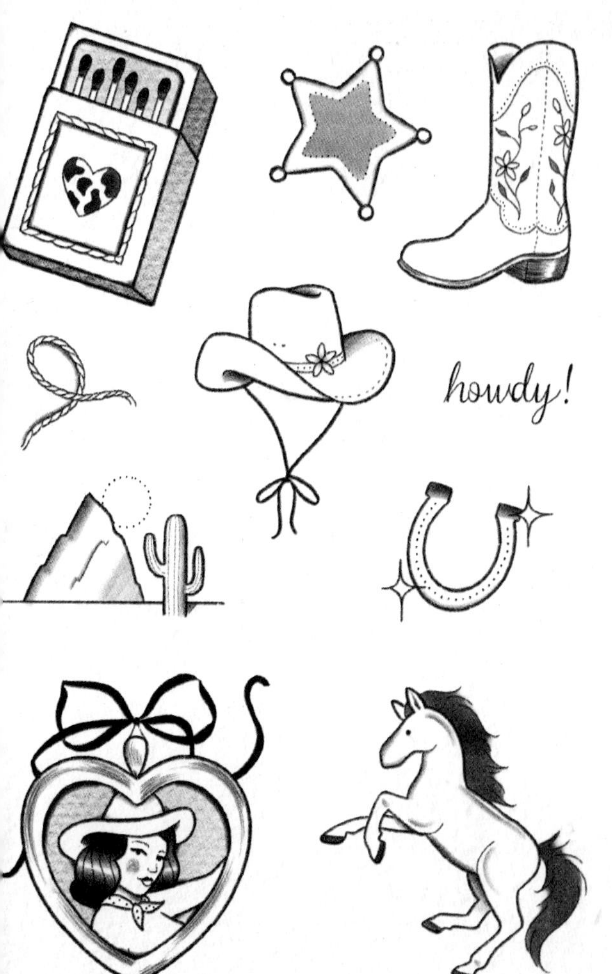

howdy!

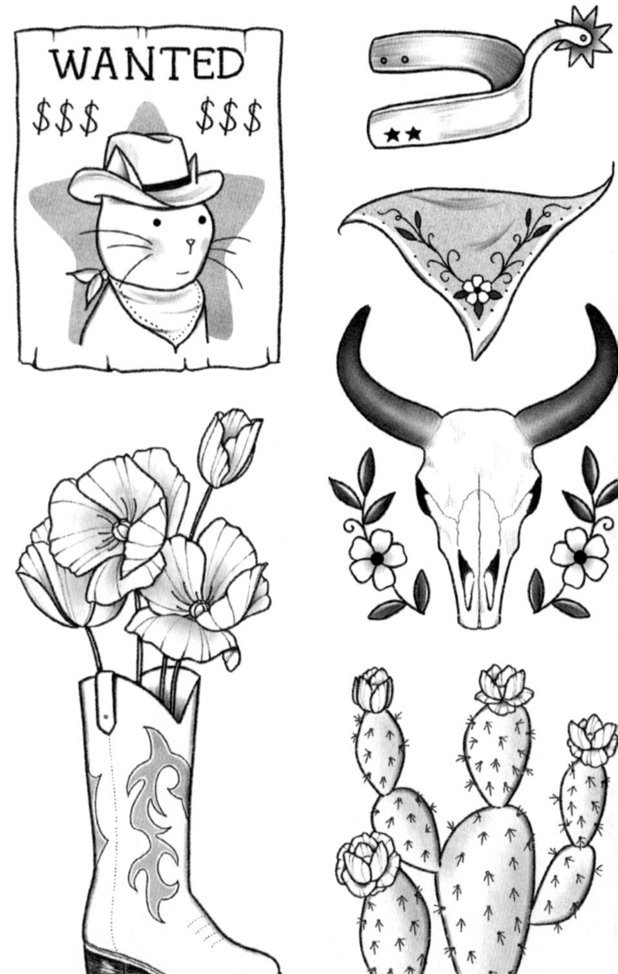
WANTED
$$$ $$$

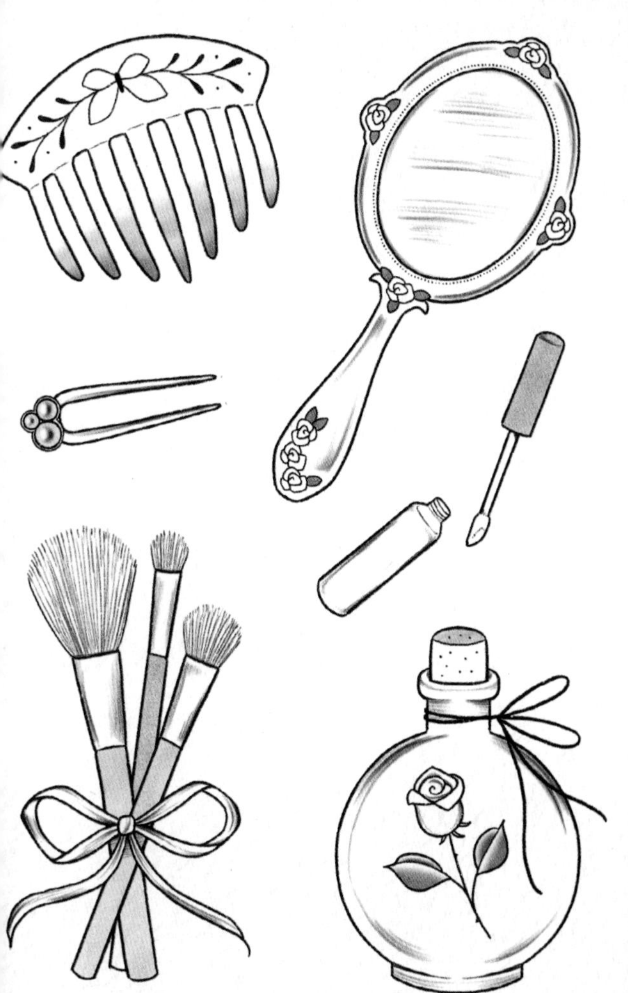

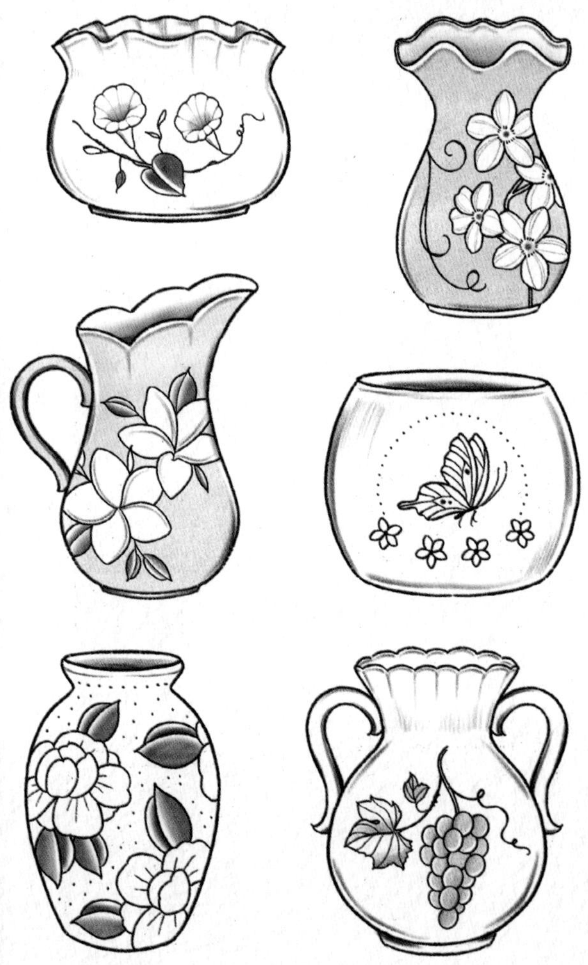

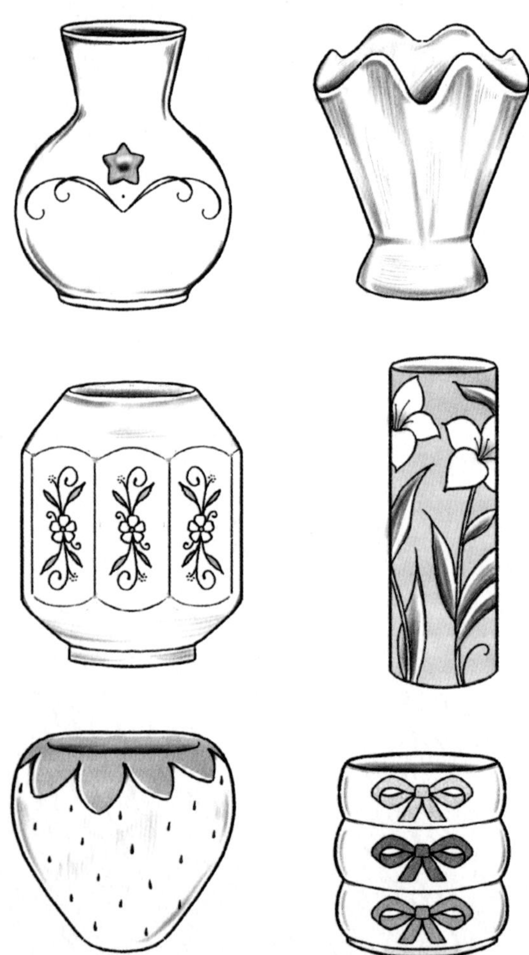

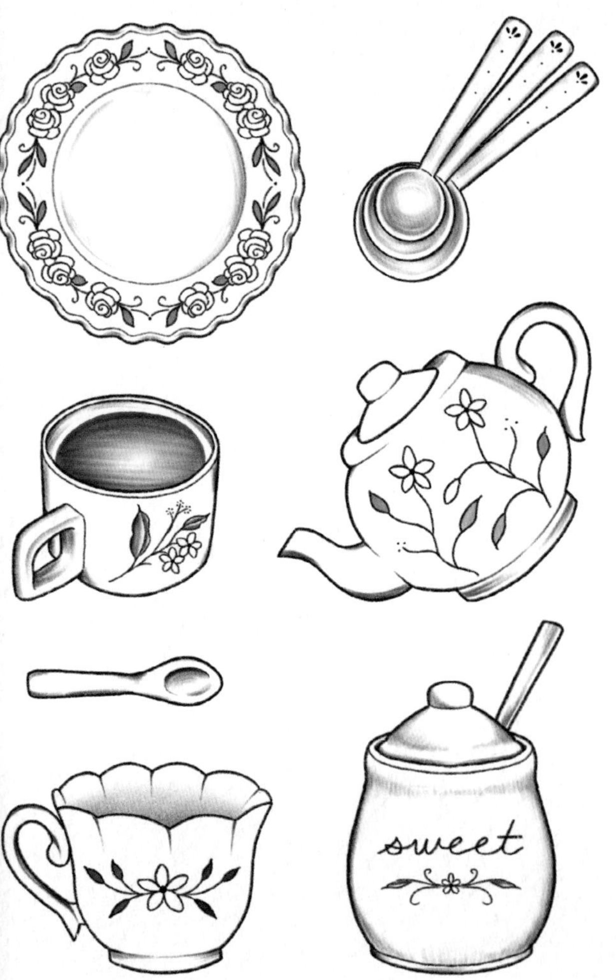

sweet

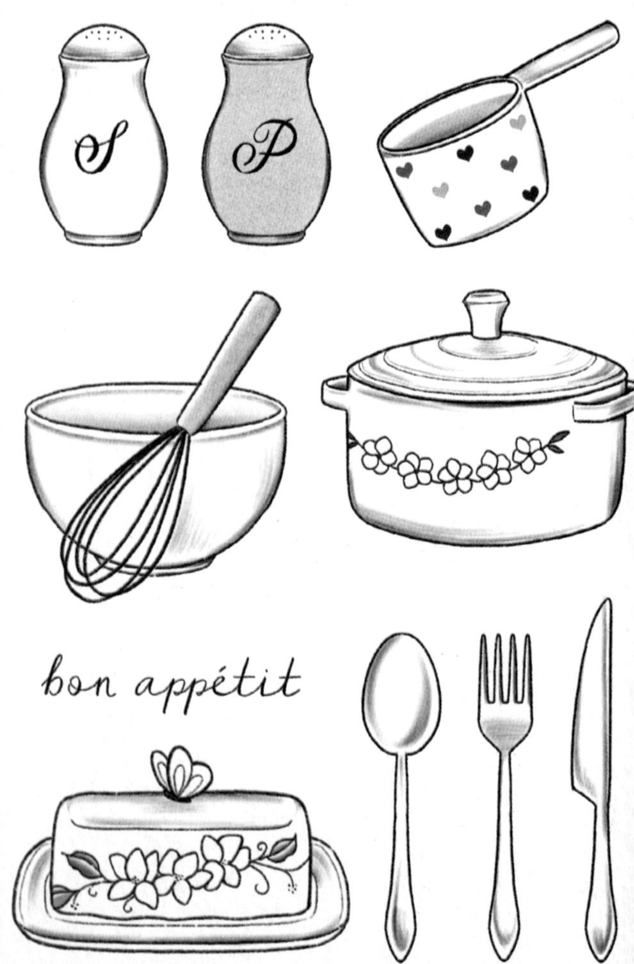
bon appétit

love
1 MSG
BFF
I <3 U
1 2 3
4 5 6
7 8 9
* 0 #

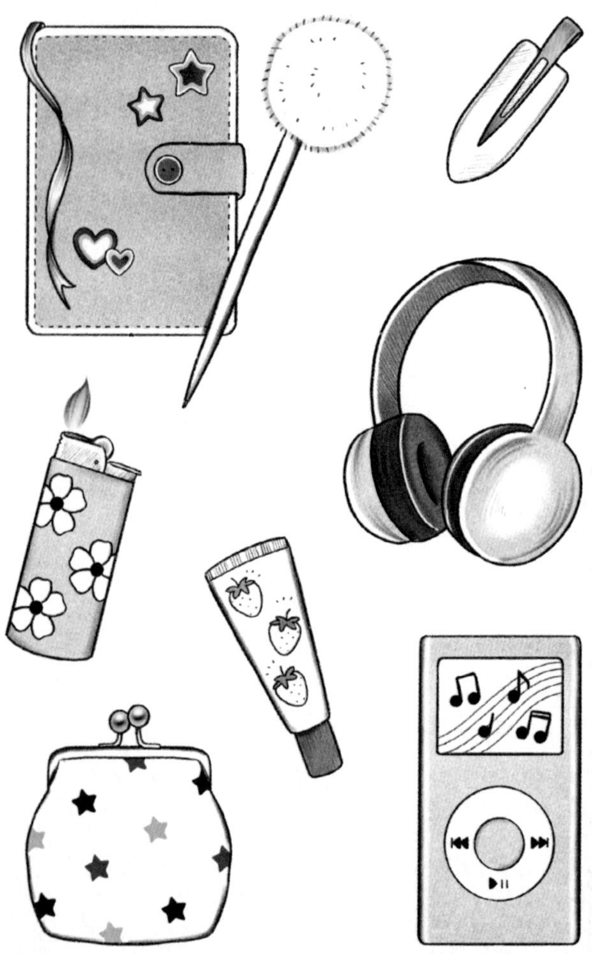

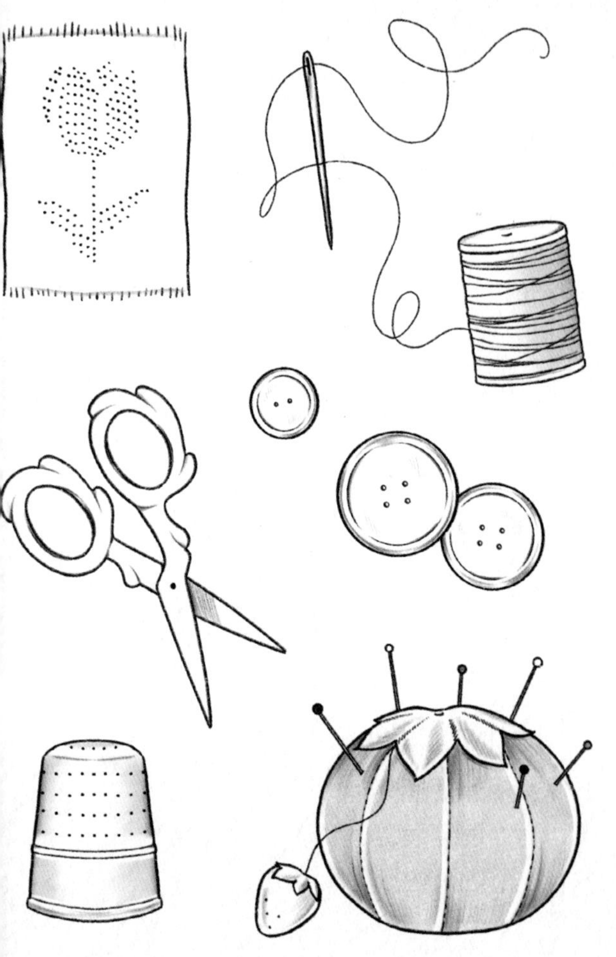

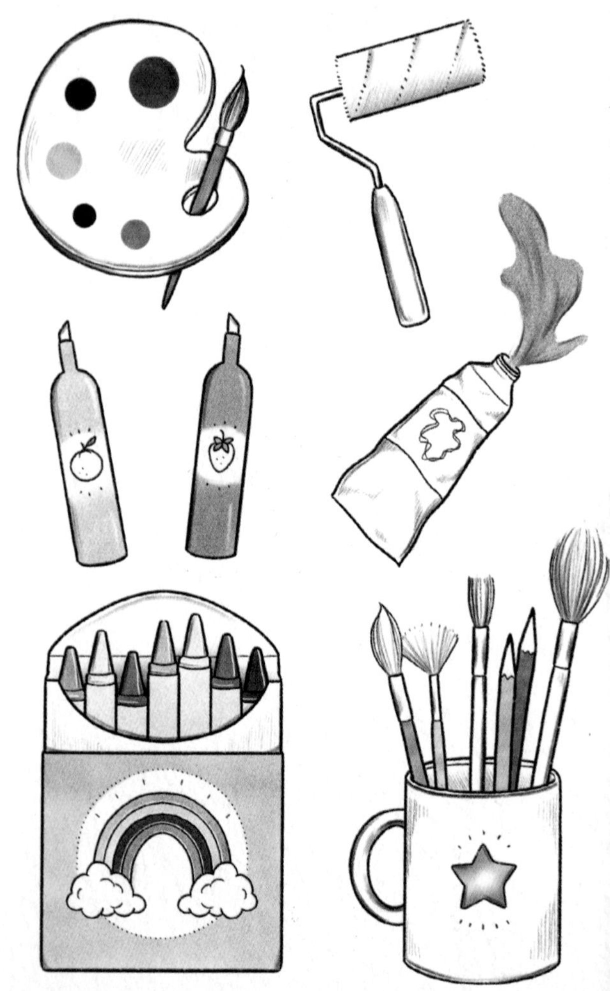

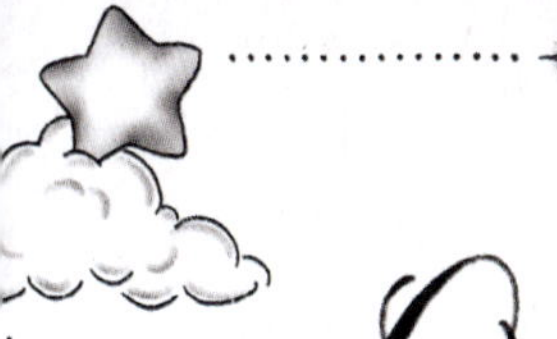
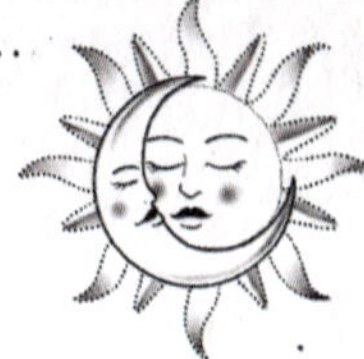

Over the Moon

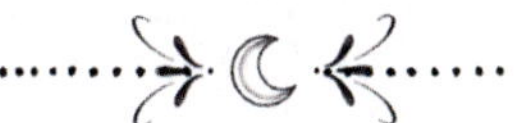

ADD A LITTLE SPARKLE TO
YOUR COLLECTION WITH THESE
TWINKLING ADORNMENTS!

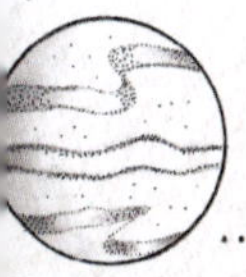
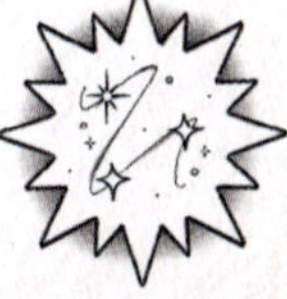

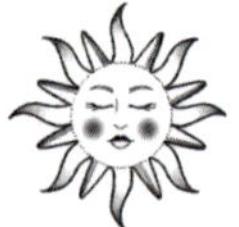

Wear your birth chart on your sleeve
(literally) with an astrology piece,
create constellations around other
tattoos, or wrap a trail of stars along
a bendy area. Consider symmetrical
placements for complementary
pieces: a sun and moon on the
wrists, or matching celestial
figures on the shoulders.

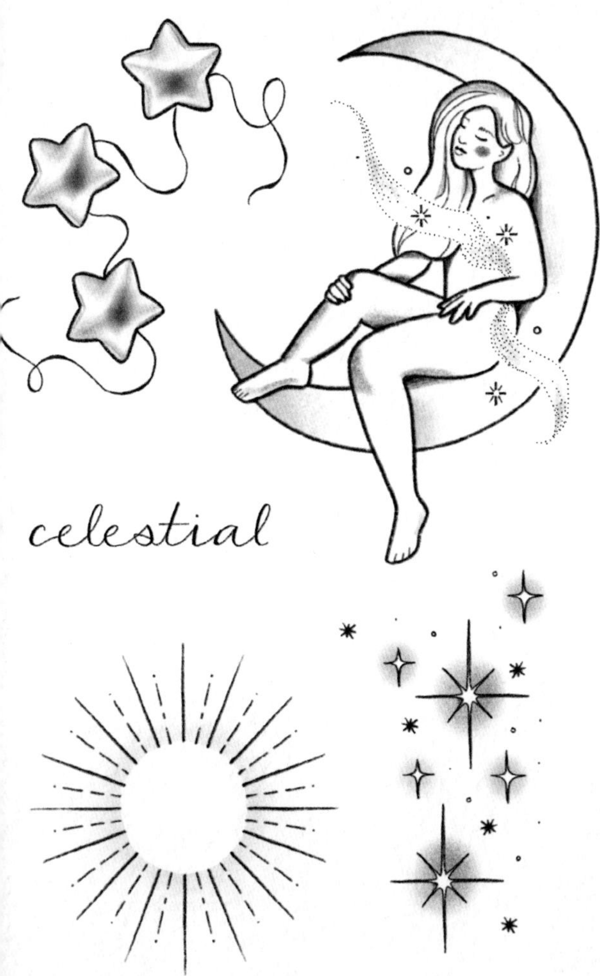

celestial

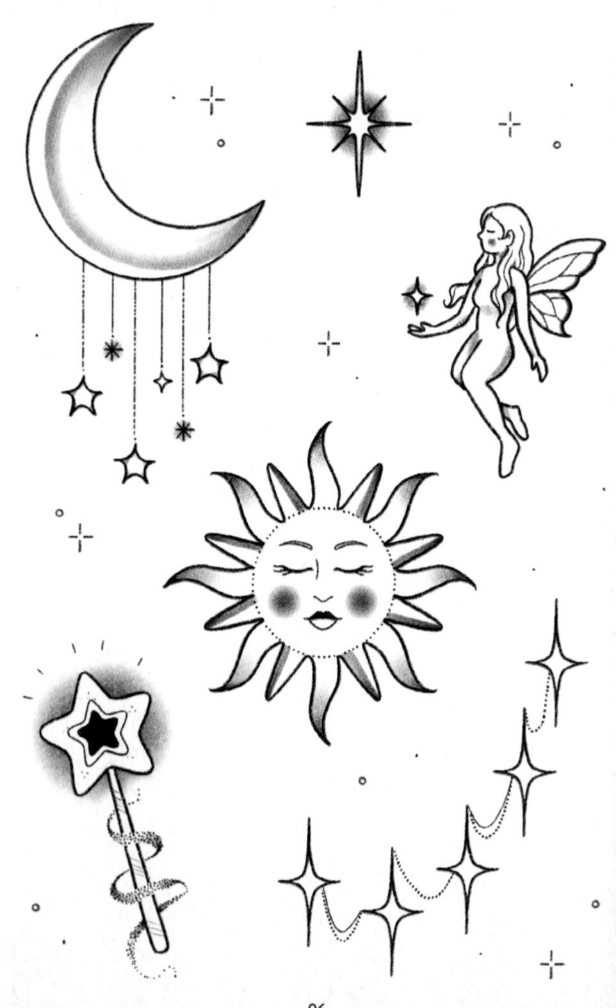

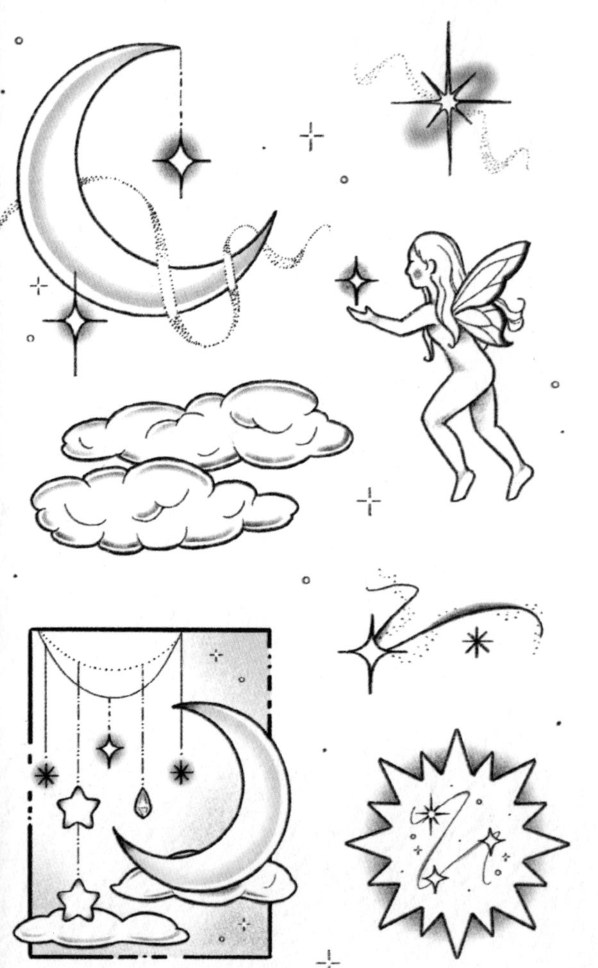

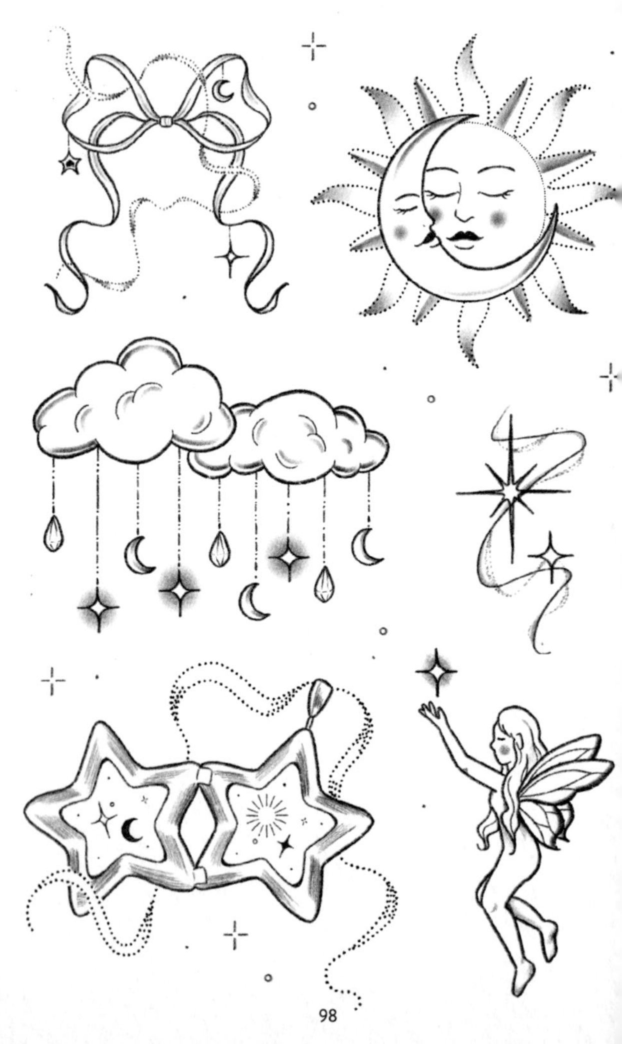

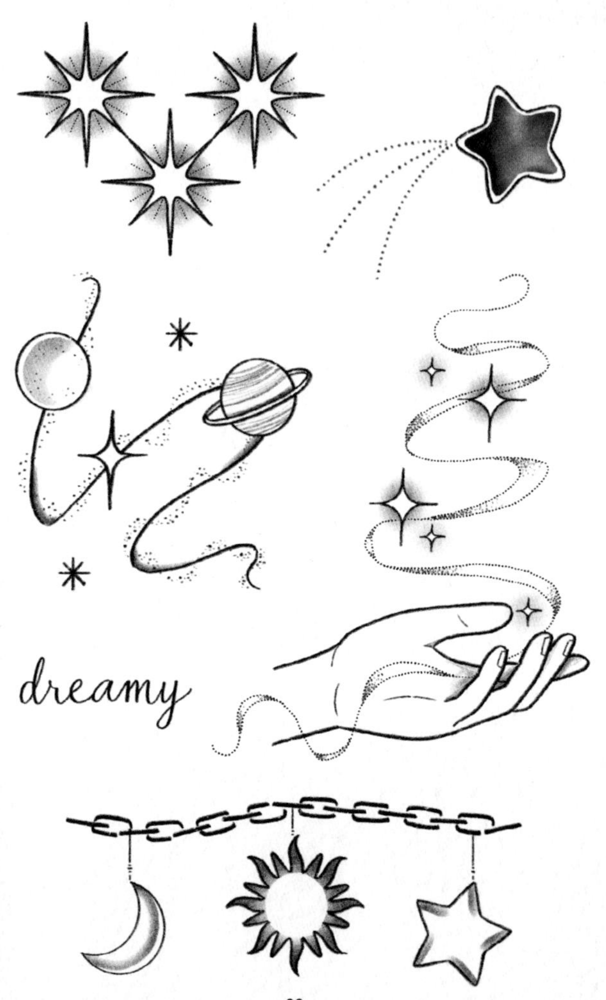

dreamy

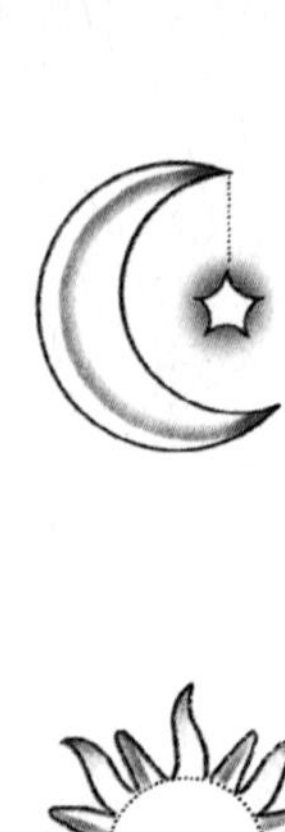

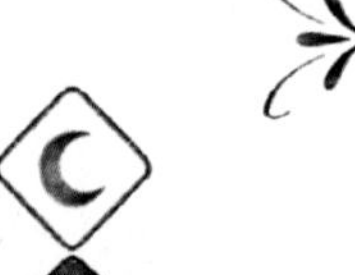

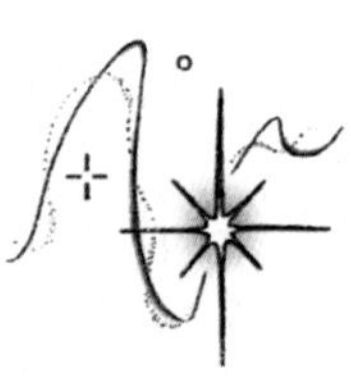
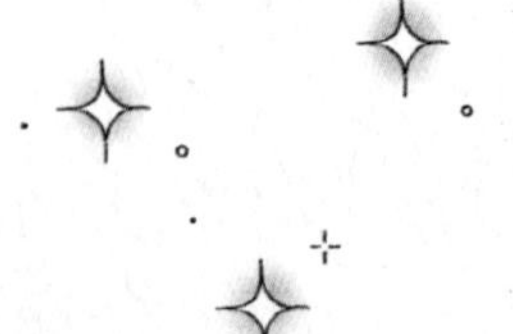
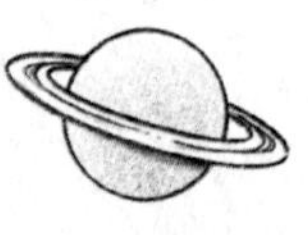

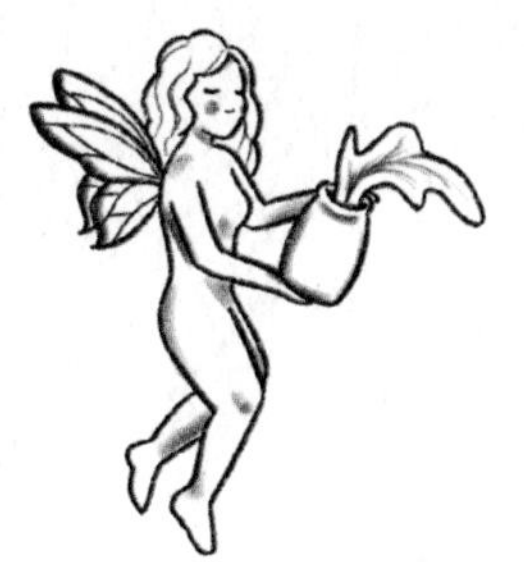

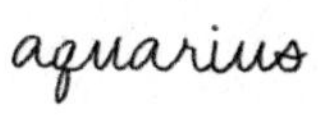
aquarius

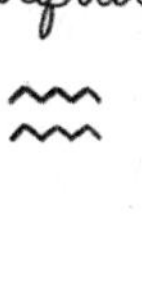

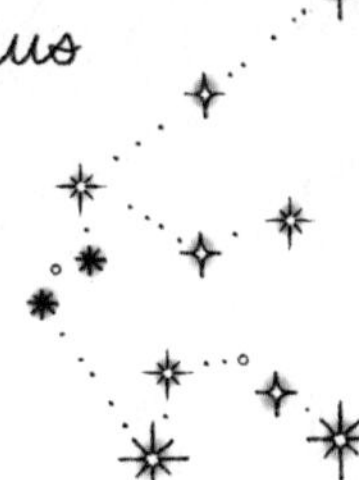

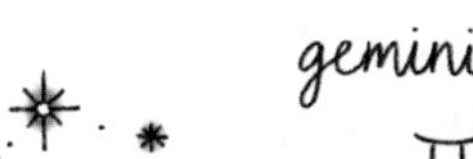
gemini

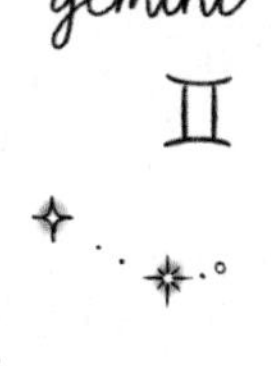

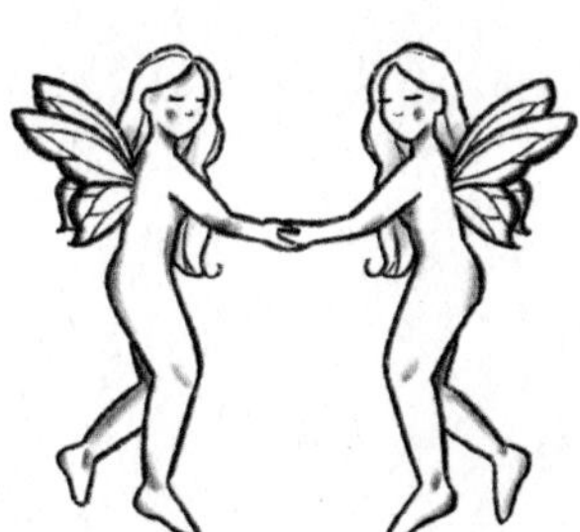

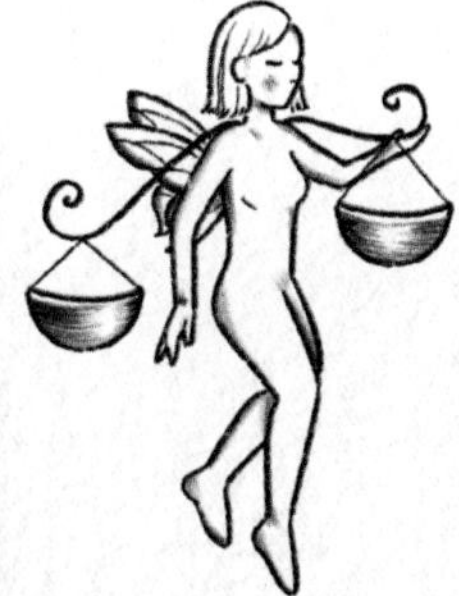

libra

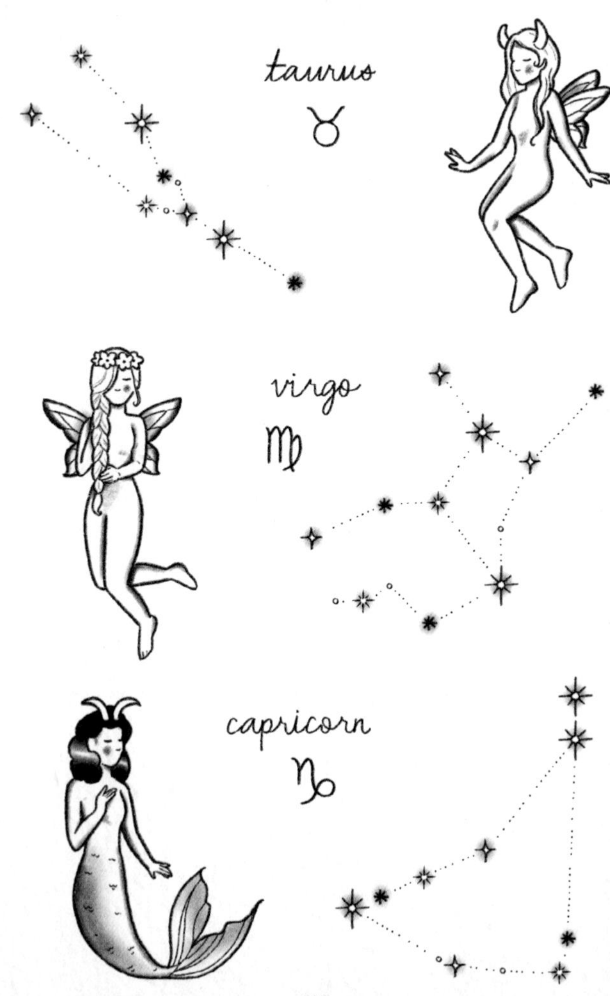

taurus
virgo
capricorn

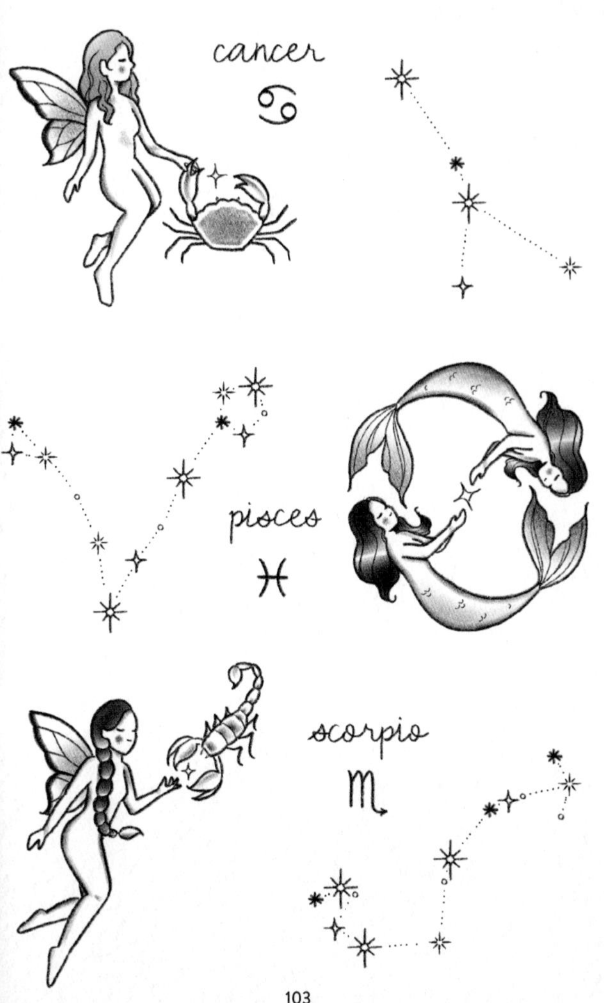

cancer
pisces
scorpio

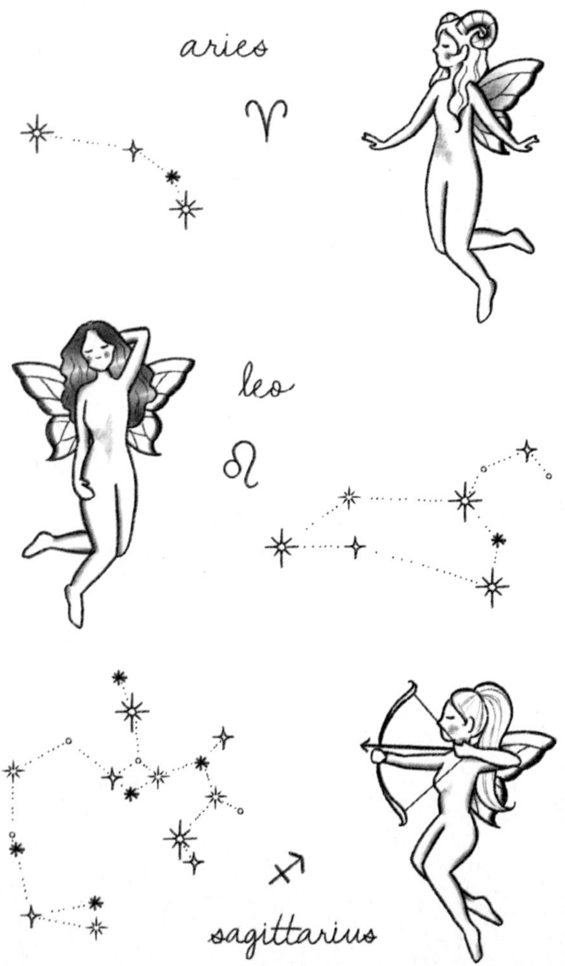

aries
leo
sagittarius
104

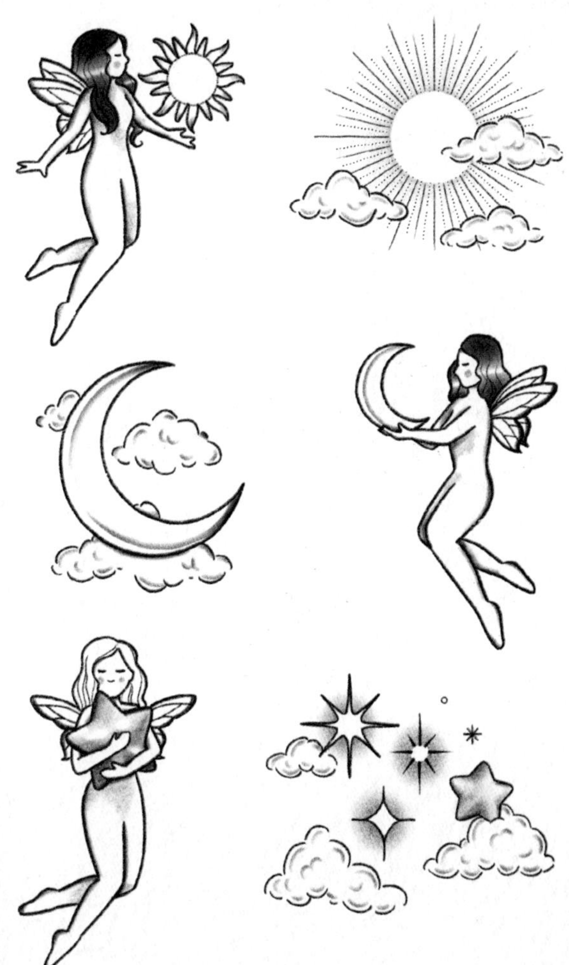

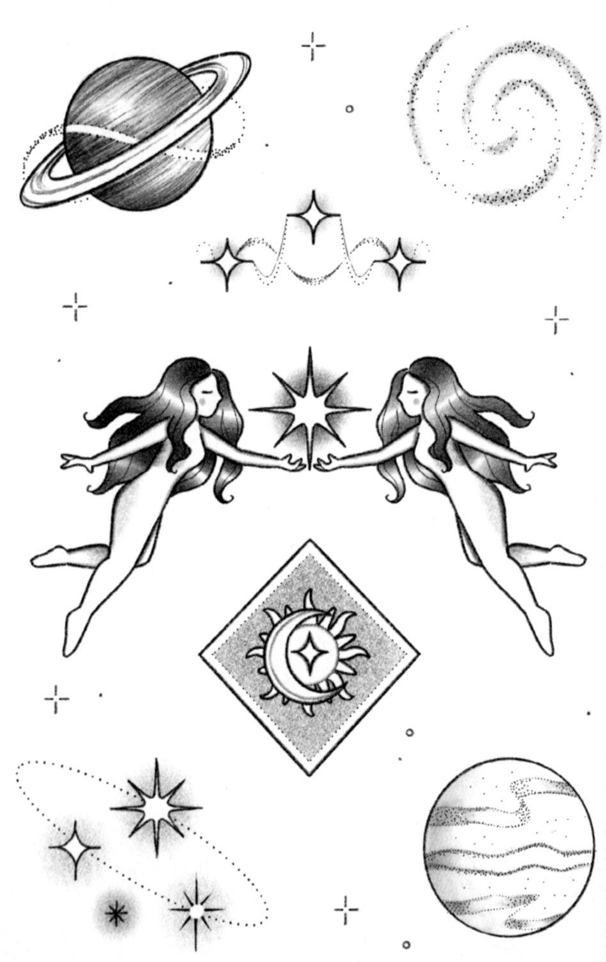

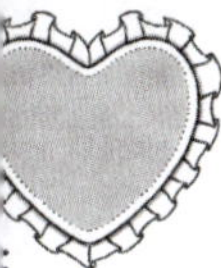

Love Me, Love Me Not

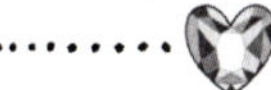

ALL THINGS HEART SHAPED
AND DRAWN WITH LOVE.

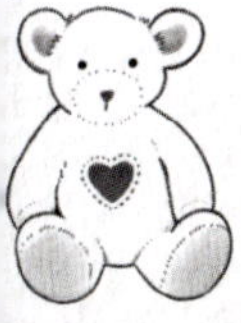

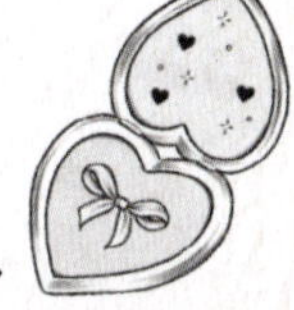

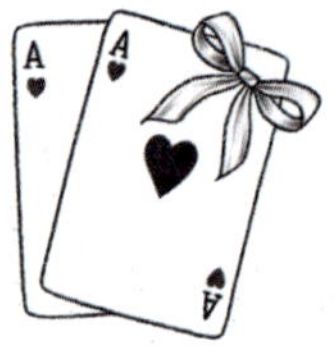

Gift yourself a permanent valentine,

or add a cheeky conversation heart

to your sticker sleeve! For pieces

you want to keep close to your heart

(but still show off), try an inner left

arm placement.

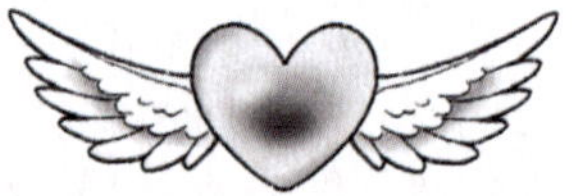

with love

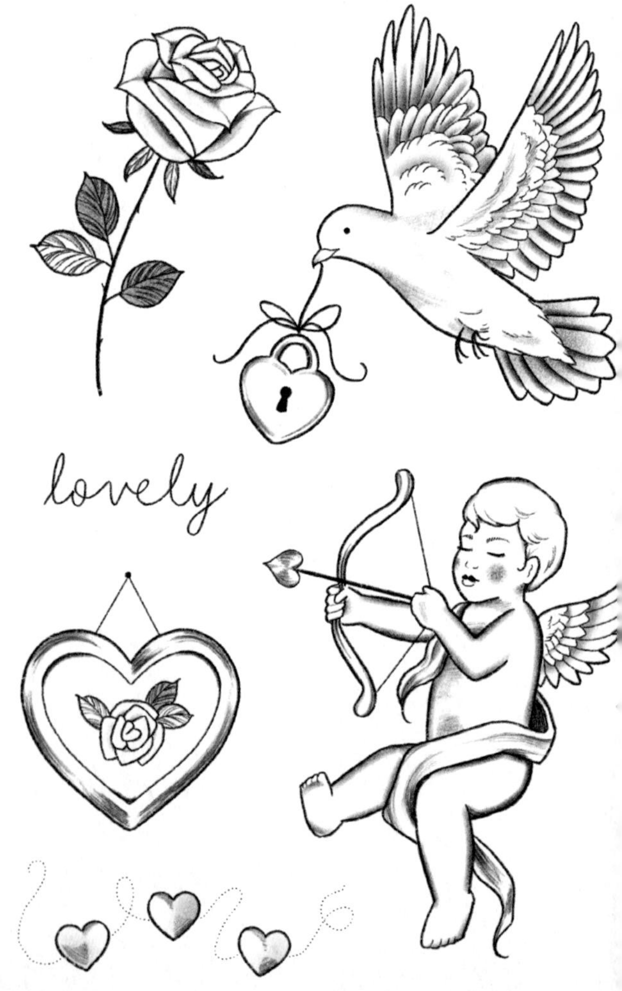
lovely

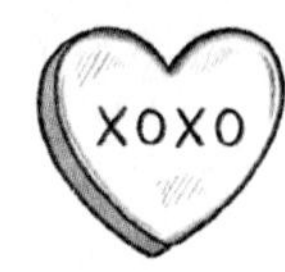
XOXO
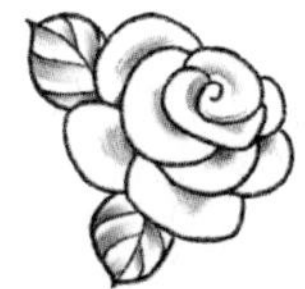
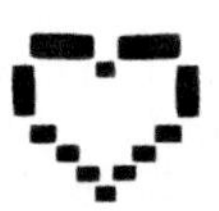

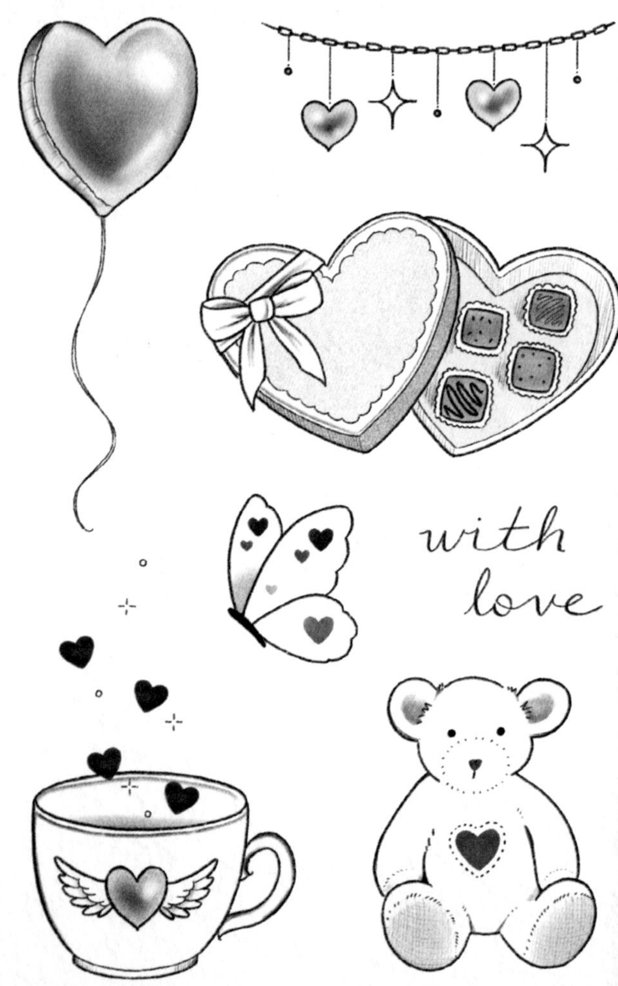
with
love

be
mine

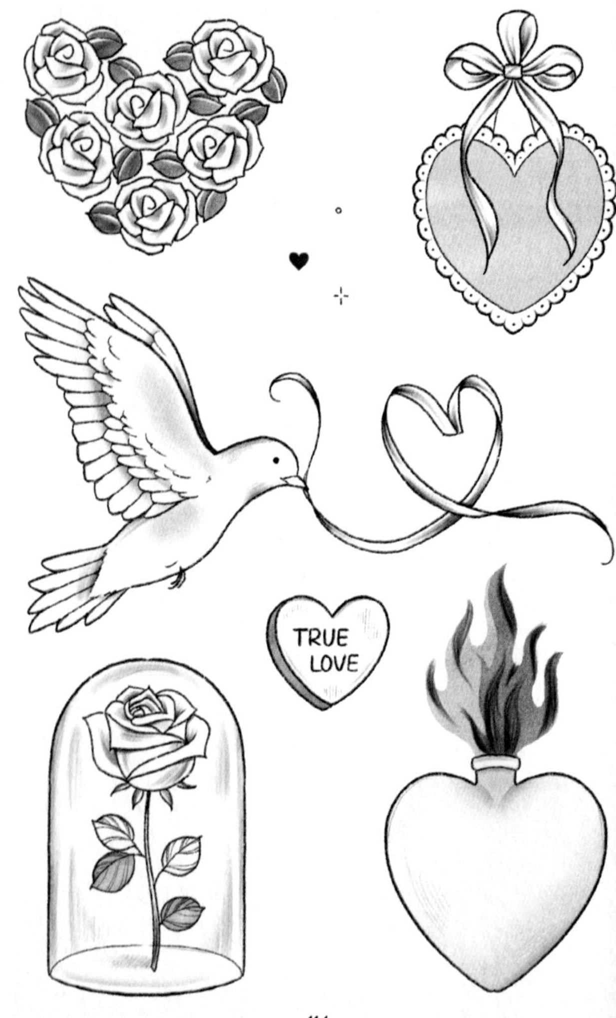

TRUE
LOVE

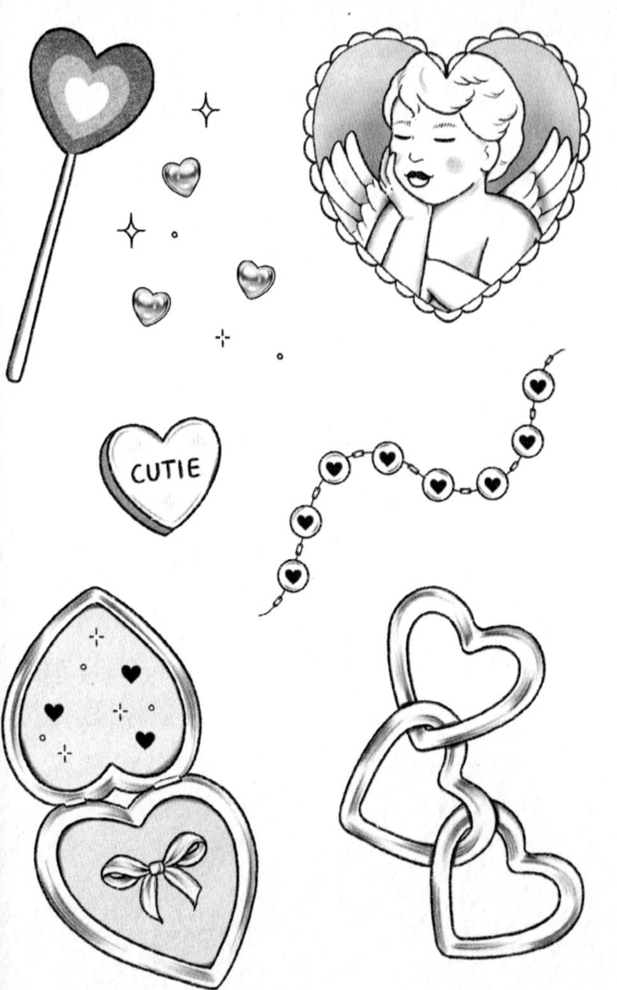

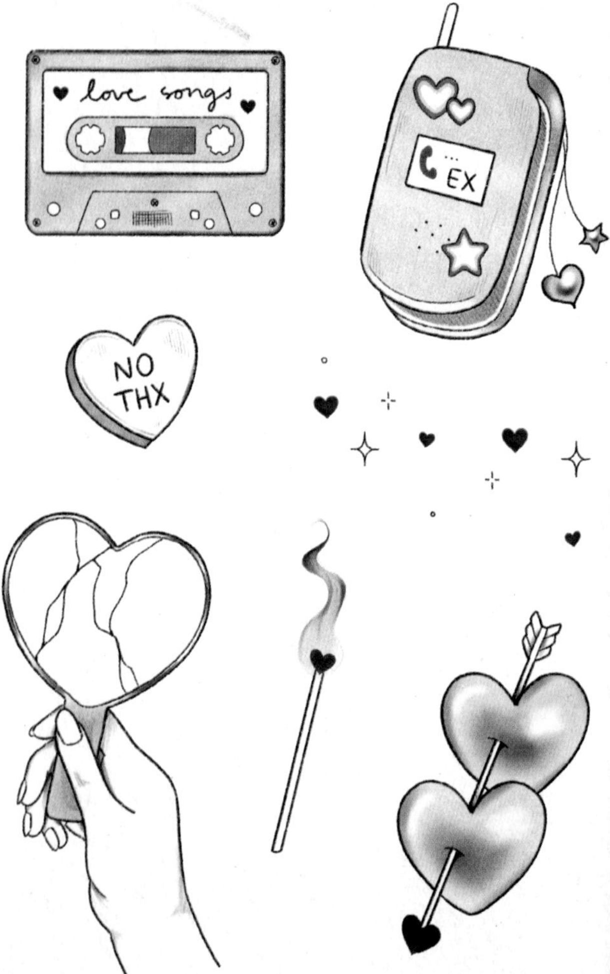

love songs
NO THX
EX

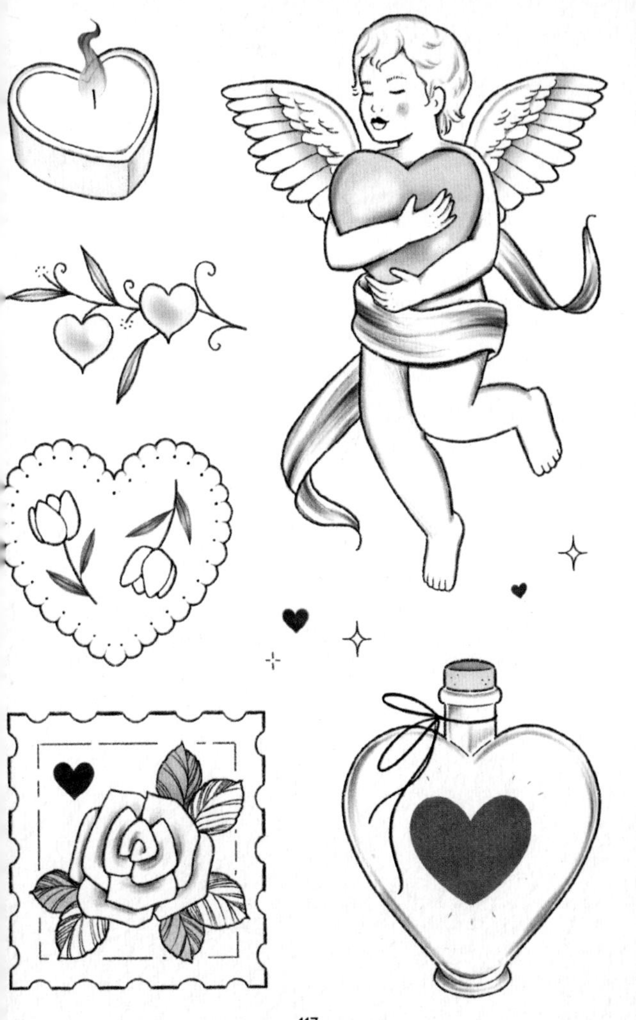

A
A
sweet

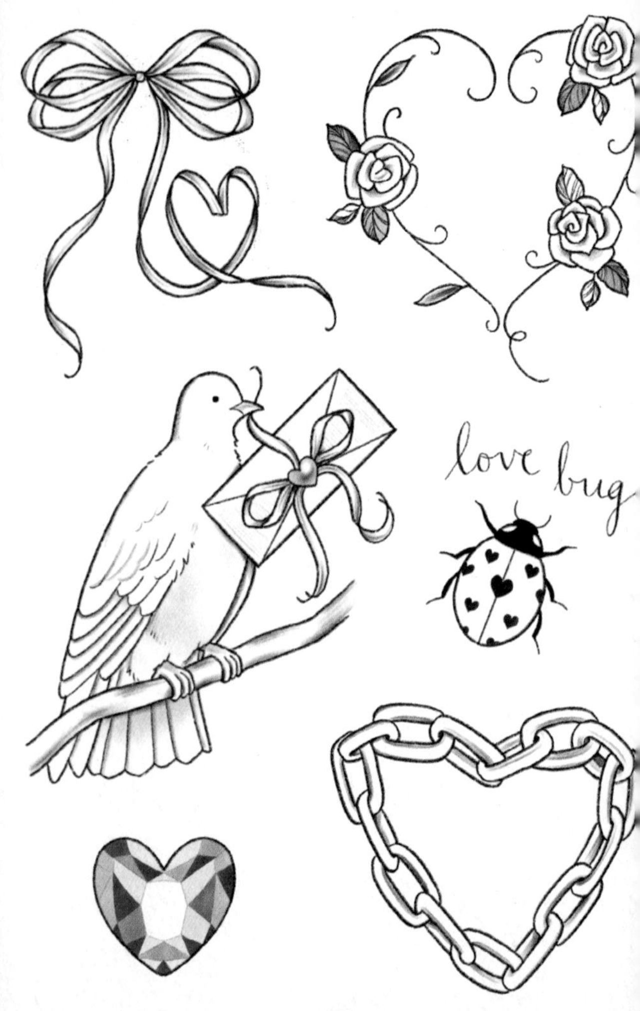

love bug

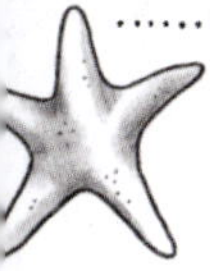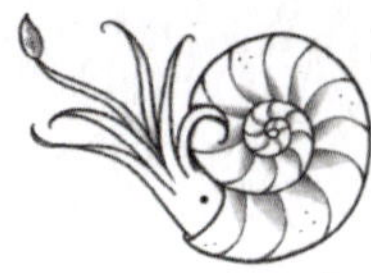

Under the Sea

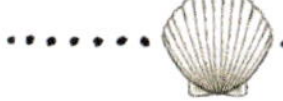

MAKE WAVES WITH AN
OCEAN-INSPIRED PIECE!

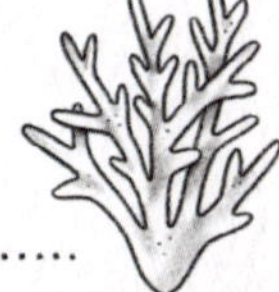

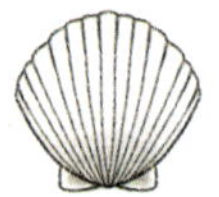

Collect a tiny seashell to remind

you of a special vacation, or add

a little mermaid for more magical

vibes. Surround these pieces with

bubbles and pearls for a complete

composition.

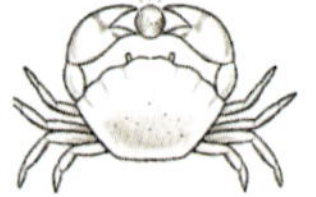

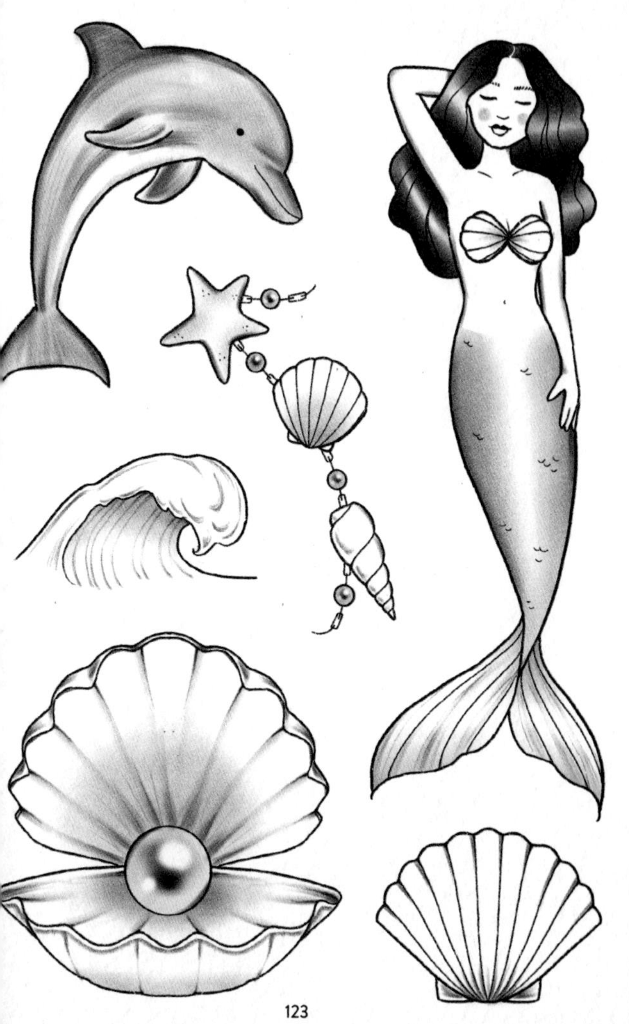

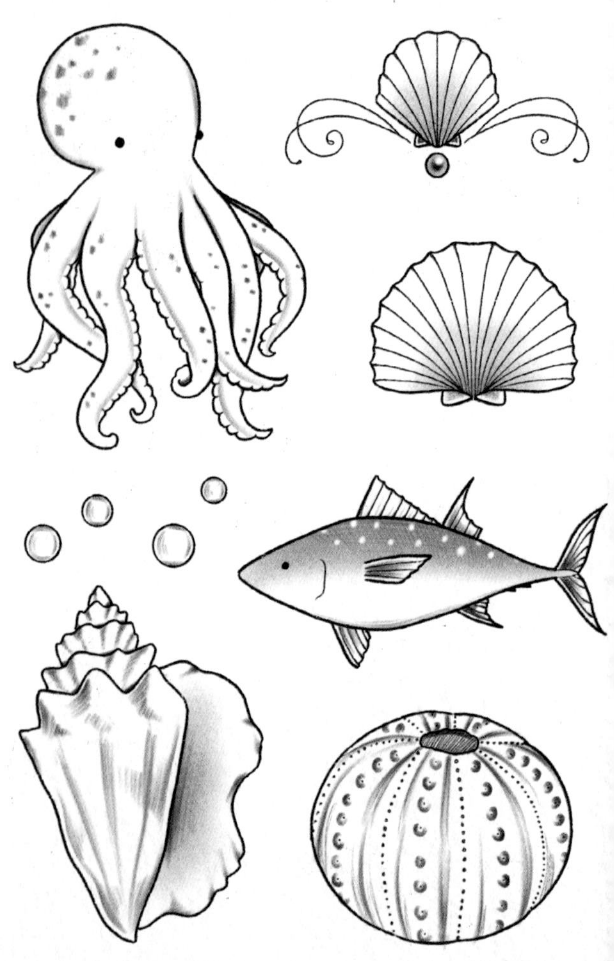

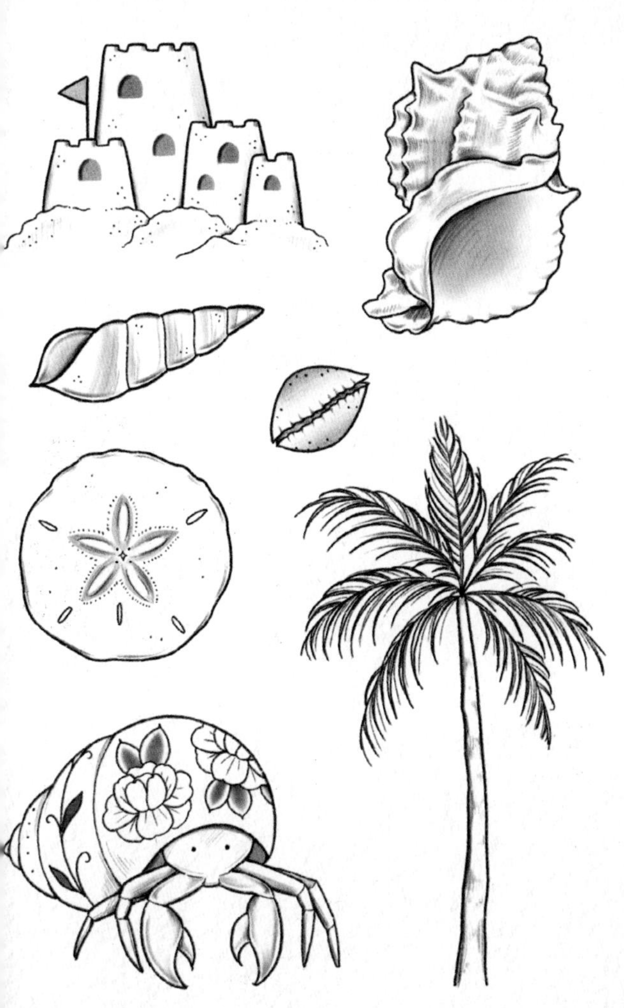

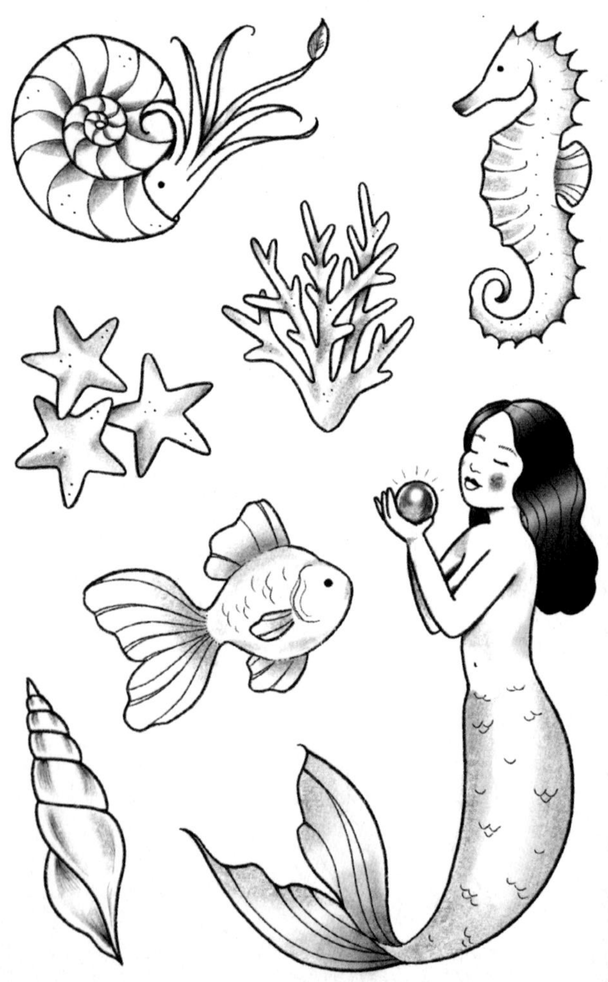

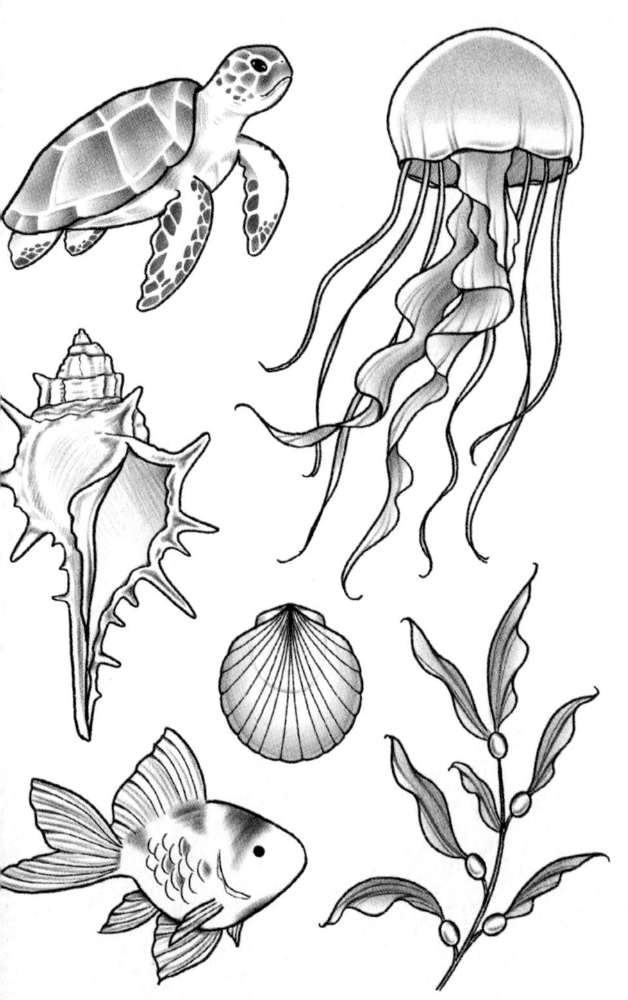

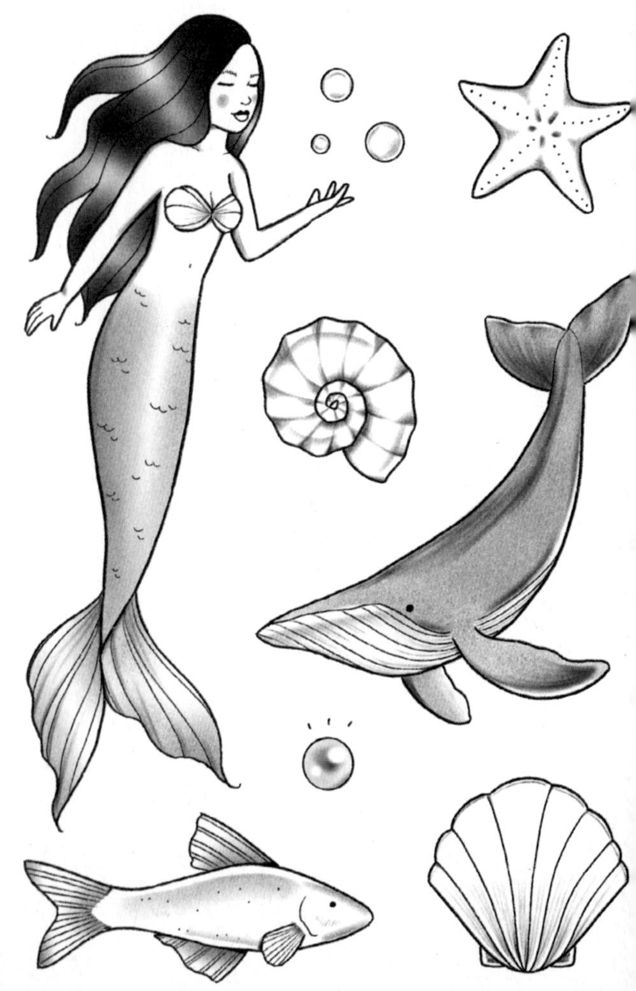

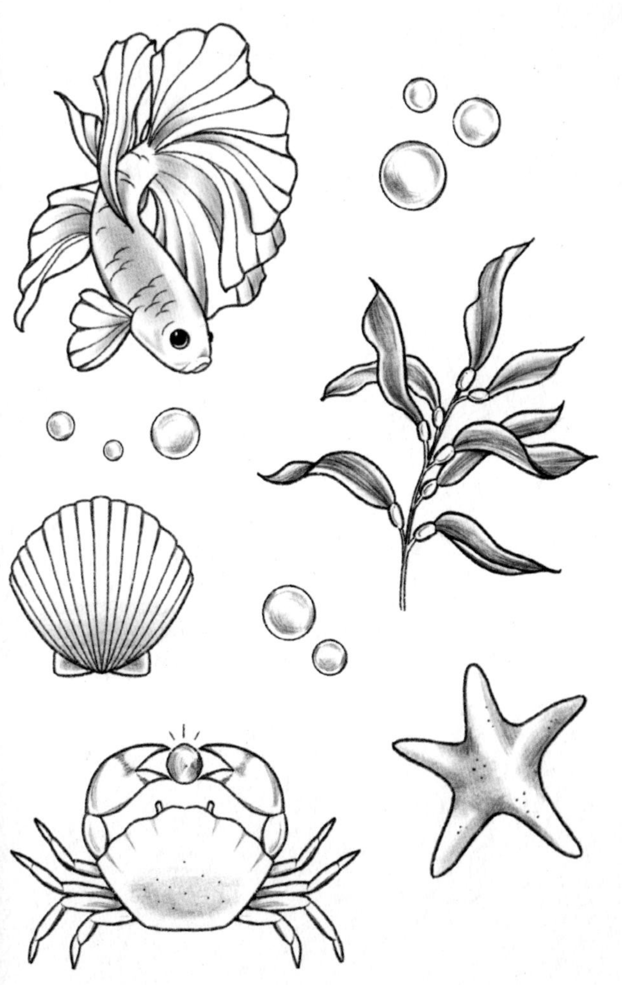

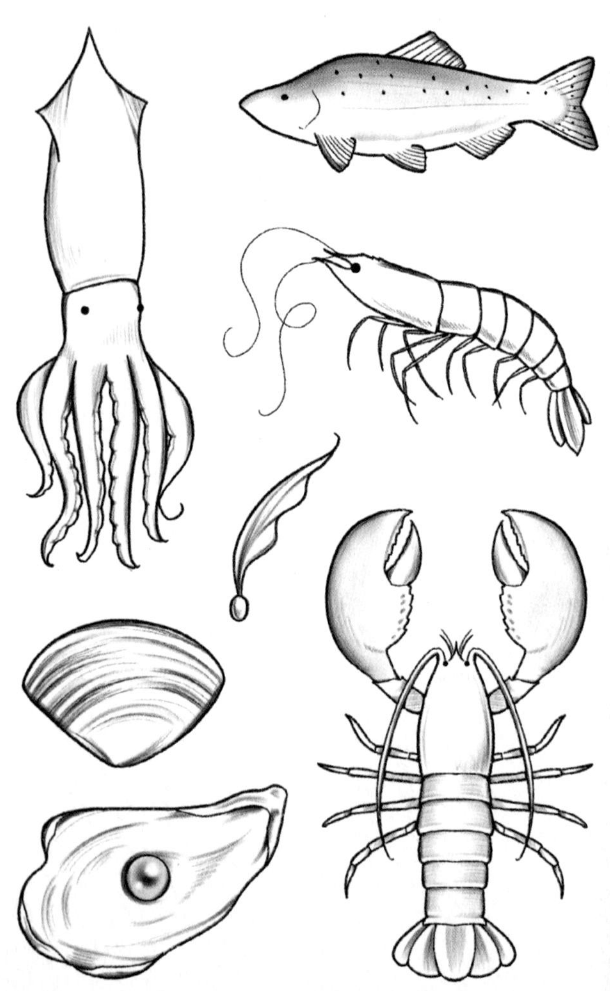

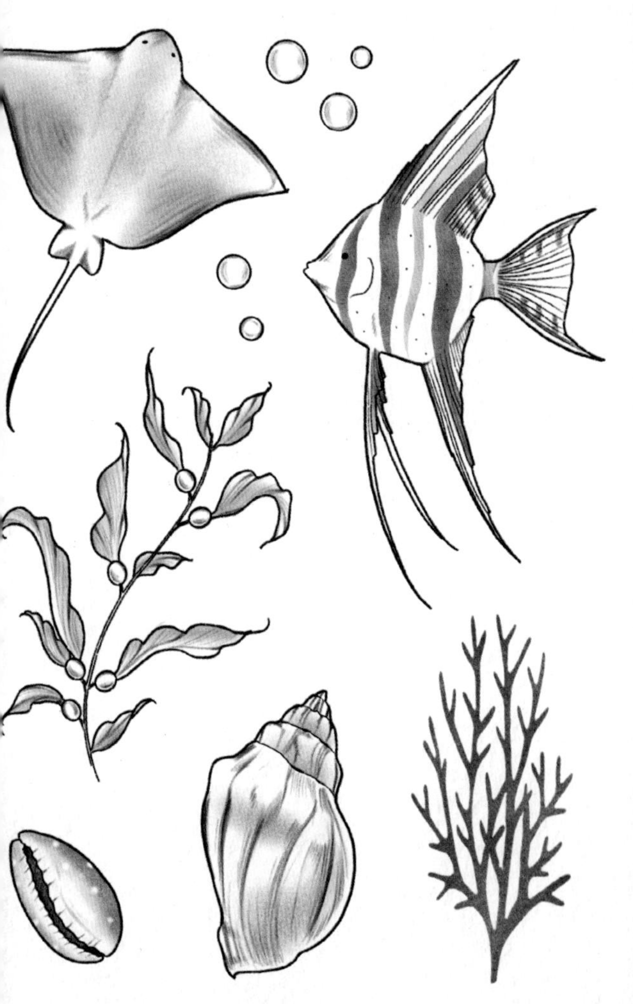

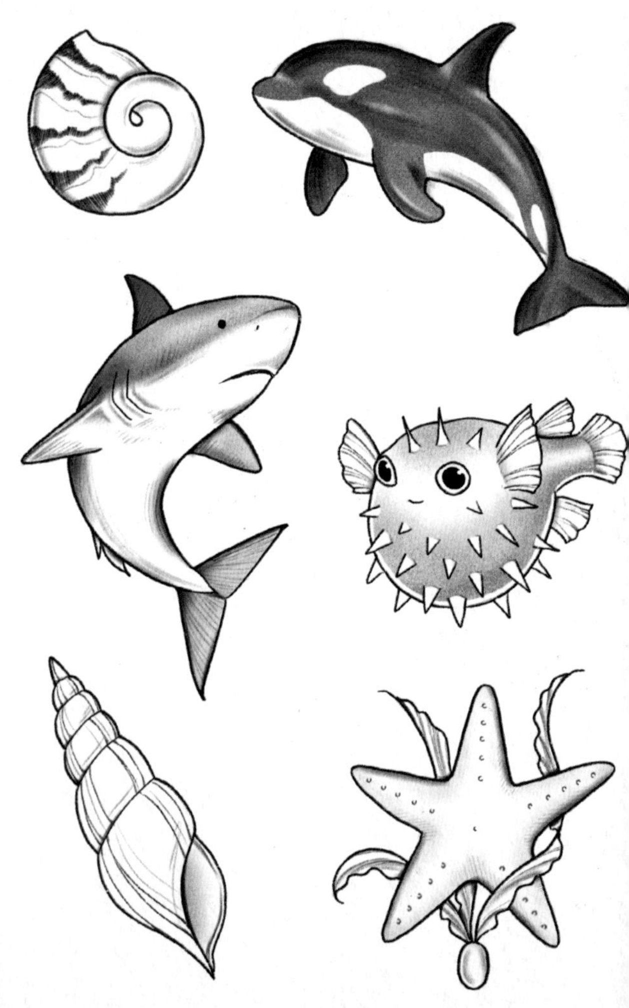

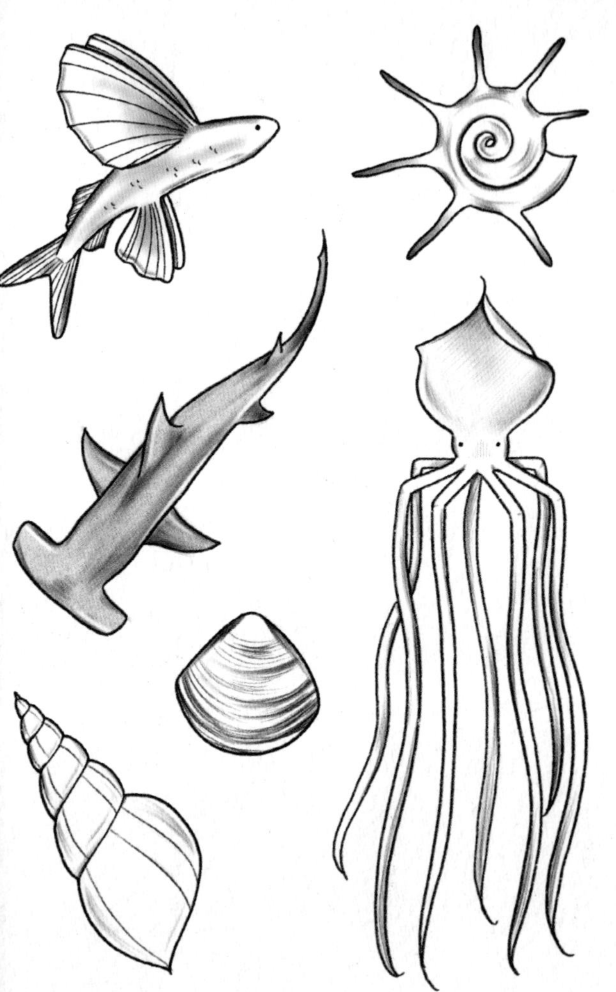

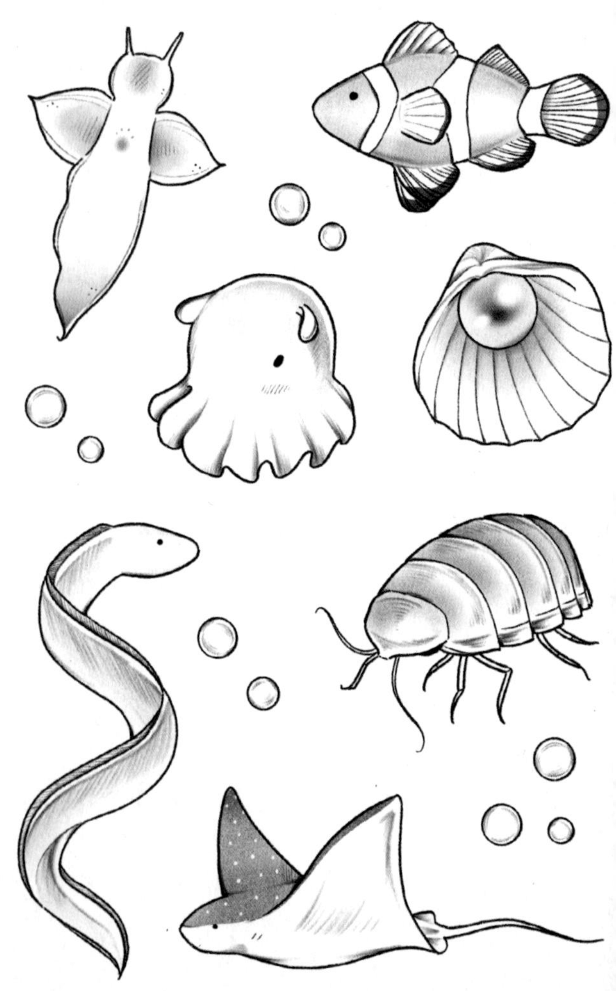

Acknowledgments

To my family, who supported my chaotic pivot from academia to the arts: Thank you for indulging my far-fetched plan to become a tattoo artist instead of going to grad school.

To my friends who have been along for the ride: Thank you for sticking around.

To the Los Angeles tattoo community: It's an honor to be here. I'm forever in awe of the creativity and artistry that surrounds me every day.

To my clients: This wouldn't be possible without you. Whether you have one tattoo from me or a whole sleeve, I'm so grateful for the opportunity to bring your ideas to life.

Finally, to my teachers: Thank you for believing in me. It was a privilege to learn to write and draw in your classrooms, and your encouragement gave me the confidence to take on a project like this.

About the Author

McKenna Lah is a Los Angeles–based fine-line tattoo artist with six years of shop experience. Her tattoo journey began while she was in college, drawing small flash designs between classes. Desperate to escape unpaid internships and grad school applications, she poured her energy into her art, focusing on all things cute and whimsical. Since then, she's built a career out of drawing things that make her happy. She hopes you enjoyed browsing these designs as much as she enjoyed creating them!

McKenna can be found at @pokingyou.softly.

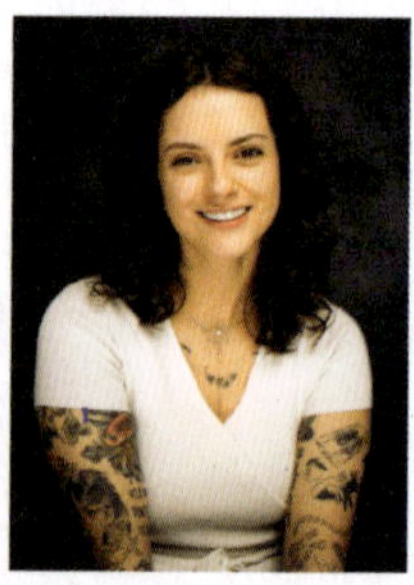

Photo by Erick Matus.

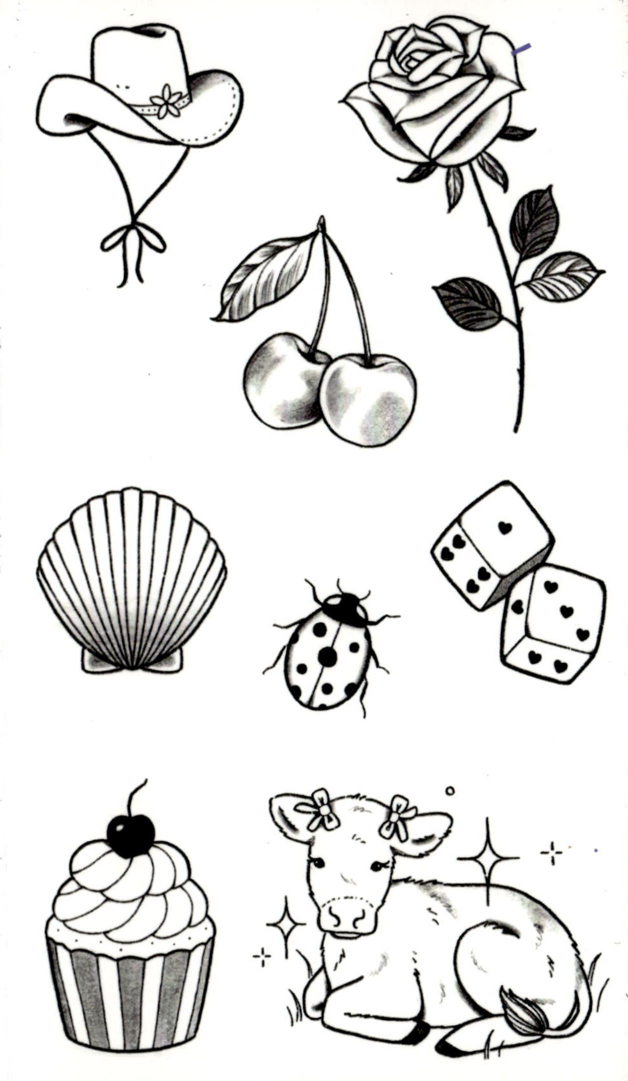

APPLYING YOUR TATTOO

1. Clean and dry the skin completely.
2. Cut out the design and remove the transparent film.
3. Apply the tattoo firmly face down, adhesive side to skin.
4. Wet the back of the tattoo with a damp cloth, making sure the entire tattoo is covered. Apply pressure evenly and wait 30–40 seconds.
5. Lift a corner to see if the tattoo is releasing. If it's not ready yet, re-wet and press down again. Once the tattoo has transferred, slide the paper away and smooth down the ends of the tattoo.
6. Rinse the tattoo gently with warm water to remove excess glue.
7. Allow the tattoo to dry. It will last several days.

REMOVING YOUR TATTOO

The tattoo will fade away within a few days. To remove it sooner, apply baby oil, vegetable oil, or lotion to the tattoo. Leave the oil or lotion on for about 30 seconds, then gently rub the tattoo with your fingers or a washcloth.

INGREDIENTS

Ethylene / VA Copolymer, Butyl Acrylate, Genipin, Water (Aqua), Rosin, Glycine Soja (Soybean) Oil, Mineral Oil (Paraffinum Liquidum), Synthetic Wax, Manganese Octanoate, D&C Black No. 2 (CI 77266), CI 74160.

CAUTION

DO NOT apply to sensitive or broken skin or around your eyes.

DO NOT ingest.

FOR AGES 12 AND UP. These tattoos are intended for adult use. Children should not use them without adult supervision, and children younger than 3 years old should not use them at all.

The sellers and manufacturers of these tattoos are not liable for any injury, loss, or damage resulting from the use of this product.

Best used before the end of March 2027.

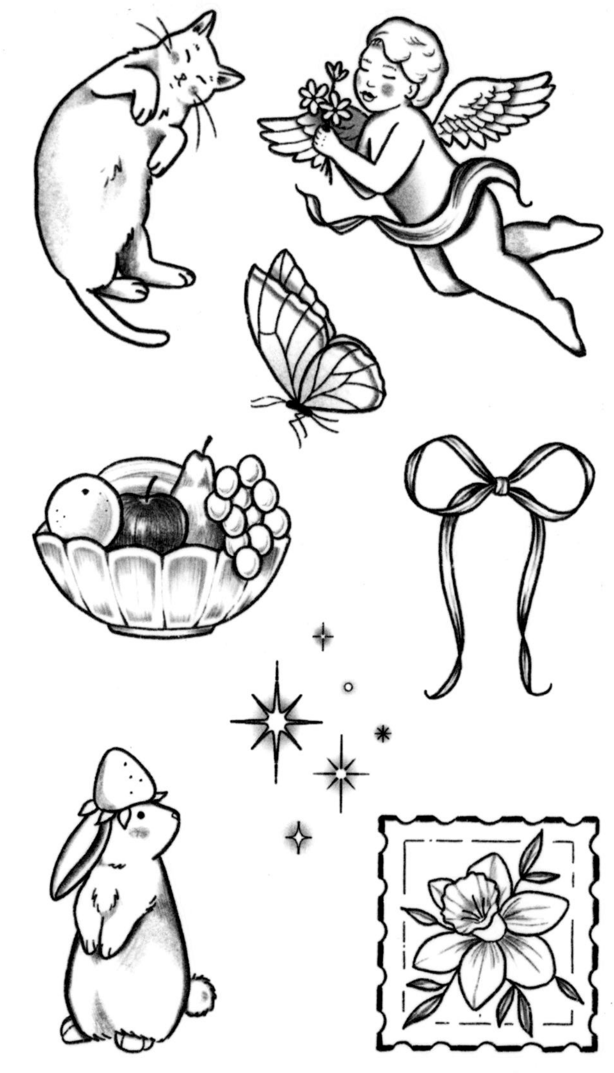

APPLYING YOUR TATTOO

1. Clean and dry the skin completely.

2. Cut out the design and remove the transparent film.

3. Apply the tattoo firmly face down, adhesive side to skin.

4. Wet the back of the tattoo with a damp cloth, making sure the entire tattoo is covered. Apply pressure evenly and wait 30–40 seconds.

5. Lift a corner to see if the tattoo is releasing. If it's not ready yet, re-wet and press down again. Once the tattoo has transferred, slide the paper away and smooth down the ends of the tattoo.

6. Rinse the tattoo gently with warm water to remove excess glue.

7. Allow the tattoo to dry. It will last several days.

REMOVING YOUR TATTOO

The tattoo will fade away within a few days. To remove it sooner, apply baby oil, vegetable oil, or lotion to the tattoo. Leave the oil or lotion on for about 30 seconds, then gently rub the tattoo with your fingers or a washcloth.

INGREDIENTS

Ethylene / VA Copolymer, Butyl Acrylate, Genipin, Water (Aqua), Rosin, Glycine Soja (Soybean) Oil, Mineral Oil (Paraffinum Liquidum), Synthetic Wax, Manganese Octanoate, D&C Black No. 2 (CI 77266), CI 74160.

CAUTION

DO NOT apply to sensitive or broken skin or around your eyes.

DO NOT ingest.

FOR AGES 12 AND UP. These tattoos are intended for adult use. Children should not use them without adult supervision, and children younger than 3 years old should not use them at all.

The sellers and manufacturers of these tattoos are not liable for any injury, loss, or damage resulting from the use of this product.

Best used before the end of March 2027.